The Laggan Redshanks

The Highland Scots in West Ulster, 1569-1630

Barry R McCain

Ulster Heritage Publishing
PO Box 884
Oxford, Mississippi 38655
USA

ISBN 978-0-9855876-2-8

Acknowledgments

Thanks to Dr William Roulston for his assistance in locating primary sources.

Preface

The Redshank settlement in the Laggan took place in the tumultuous years during the sixteenth century that were dominated by Elizabethan English attempts to bring Ulster firmly under the control of the Crown. The Redshanks were vital players in the affairs of those times and indeed it was their military skills that delayed the conquest of Ulster until the beginning of the next century. The story of the Laggan Redshanks is often overshadowed in the ebb and flow of epic events that took place in the seventeenth century, namely the Plantation of Ulster. In Donegal the close relationship between west Ulster and the Scottish Gaeltacht is better known, because it is a living part of daily life there. It is found in the surnames of many Donegal folk and in the dialect of Gaelic spoken there. The story of the Laggan Redshanks has many fascinating elements which include Clann Chaimbeul and their dynamic leader the fifth Earl of Argyll, Gaelic sexual intrigues, English Machiavellian manoeuvres, and the Redshanks themselves.

Note to Reader

The Gaelic spellings in the text are in modern Irish Gaelic orthography with some Ulster and Argyll dialect influences. Gaelic is used as a general label for the Goidelic language of Ireland and Scotland. 'Irish' is used interchangeably with 'Gaelic' when referencing language. Gaelic forms of personal names are used in many cases when referring to people prior to 1600, because of the complete inconsistency of anglicised forms. Geographic names follow the orthography of modern Ordnance Survey maps in most cases.

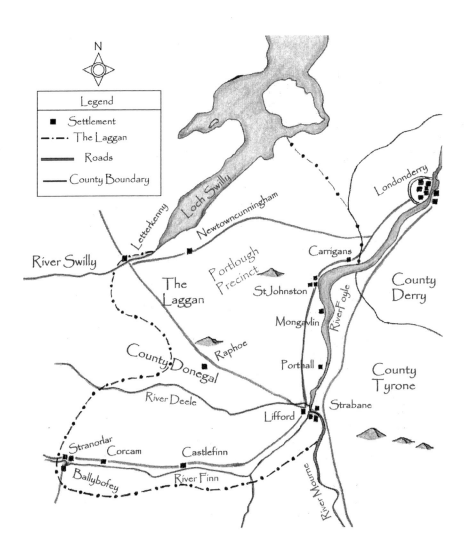

N

Legend

■ Settlement
·—·—· The Laggan
▬▬▬ Roads
—— County Boundary

Loch Swilly

Londonderry

Letterkenny

River Swilly

Newtowncunningham

Carrigans

Portlough
Precinct

St Johnston

County
Derry

The
Laggan

River Foyle

Mongavlin

Raphoe

County Donegal

Porthall

County
Tyrone

River Deele

Lifford

Strabane

Stranorlar

Corcam

Castlefinn

Ballybofey

River Finn

River Mourne

iv

Table of Contents

Dramatis Personae

Anna Mhic Dhónaill née Caimbeul The daughter of the third Earl of Argyll. She married her second husband, Seamus Mac Dónaill of Dunnyveg and the Glens, in 1545, forming an alliance between the Houses of Caimbeul and Mac Dónaill. Seamus was killed by Seaán Ó Neill in 1565. Her sister, Elizabeth, married James Stewart, first Earl of Moray, who was an illegitimate son of King James IV of Scotland. Anna's daughter was Fionnuala Nic Dhónaill who married Aodh Mac Manus Ó Dónaill. Anna's third husband was Tarlach Luineach Ó Neill.

Aodh Rua Ó Dónaill The taoiseach (chief) of Clann Uí Dhónaill. He was the oldest son of Fionnuala Nic Dhónaill and a central figure in the Nine Years War (1594-1603). He employed thousands of Redshanks.

Catríona Nic Ghiolla Eáin The daughter of Eachann Mór Mac Giolla Eáin of Mull. She was the wife of the fourth Earl of Argyll and after his death the wife of Calbhach Ó Dónaill. She became the mistress and later wife of Seaán Ó Neill an díomais.

Donnchadh Caimbeul (sometimes anglicised as Dennis Campbell). He was an illegitimate son of the fifth Earl of Argyll and a bishop in the Established Church in Ireland. He proposed using the Caimbeul Redshanks living on the Foyle River to further Scottish interest in west Ulster in the early 1600s. He was appointed Bishop of Raphoe in Donegal in 1603.

Eóin Mór Mac Dónaill The brother of the second King of the Isles, Dónal Mac Dónaill. In 1399 he married Máire Nic Eóin, the daughter of Eóin Mac Eóin, and gained control of the Glens of Antrim.

Fionnuala Uí Dhónaill née Nic Dhónaill She is known in history as Iníon Dubh and was the daughter of Anna Mhic Dhónaill. She was raised in the Stewart court in Scotland. She married Aodh Mac Manus Ó Dónaill in 1569. Their oldest son was Aodh Rua Ó Dónaill, one of the Irish leaders in the Nine Years War. In the 1580s she took over leadership of Clann Uí Dhónaill due to her husband's poor health. Iníon Dubh commanded a large force of Redshanks and many of them settled in the Portlough precinct in the Laggan. Her cousins were the fifth and sixth Earls of Argyll.

Giolla Easpuig Donn Caimbeul The fifth Earl of Argyll. He succeeded to the earldom in 1558. He married Jean Stewart, the natural daughter of James V (divorced in 1564). He was a convert to the Reformed faith, but also supported Catholic lords in Ireland and Scotland and Mary Queen of Scots. He was behind the Redshank settlement in the Laggan.

Sir James Cunningham A Scottish knight and one of the original Undertakers in Portlough precinct. His uncle was James Cunningham, another Scottish Undertaker in Portlough precinct.

James McKeen A descendant of the Portlough precinct Redshanks. He was the co-leader of the 1718 fleet which began the Ulster Migration to the Colonies. He established the Scots-Irish settlement in Nutfield, New Hampshire, and served as its first magistrate.

John Stewart By 1619 an Undertaker in Portlough precinct. He is thought to be a son, possibly illegitimate, of Ludovic Stewart. After the Plantation he held Mongavlin Castle near Porthall.

Ludovic Stewart The second Duke of Lennox. He was the son of Esmé Stewart, first Duke of Lennox and Catherine de Balsac. Stewart was involved in the Plantation of Ulster in Ireland and the colonization of Maine in New England. His lands in Ulster were in the Portlough precinct.

Seaán Ó Néill (anglicised and said Shane O'Neill) He was called 'an díomais' meaning 'the Proud.' Seaán was the taoiseach of the Clann Uí Neill. He defeated Clann Dhónaill at the battle of Glentaisie in May 1565 which led to a series of events that brought the Redshanks to the Laggan in late summer of 1569.

Seamus Mac Dónaill He was the taoiseach of Clann Eóin Mhóir, also known as Clann Dhónaill. He was the second husband of Anna Chaimbeul and the father of Iníon Dubh.

Somhairle Bui Mac Dónaill (said 'Sorley Bwee') The leader of Clann Eóin Mhóir in the Glens and the Route and brother of Seamus Mac Dónaill.

Tarlach Luineach Ó Neill The chief of Clann Uí Neill. Tarlach was the tánaiste (sub chief) to Seaán Ó Neill and became the taoiseach of the clan after Seaán's death. He married Anna Mhic Dhónaill née Caimbeul, the widow of Seamus Mac Dónaill. He established the town of Strabane, County Tyrone.

1 Introduction

Readers of Scottish and Irish history are familiar with the term Redshank. In Scotland it is used as a synonym for a Highlander or an Isles man. The term was also used in Ireland to describe Scottish Gaels. In an Irish context it most often described the Scottish Gaels that came to Ireland in service of Irish lords in the 1500s and later applied to their descendants well into the 1700s. By the mid-1400s, Redshanks were crossing the North Channel to Ireland to hire out as mercenaries for the summer campaign season. After the campaign, usually mid to late fall, they returned to their homes in the Isles or the Highlands. This pattern of seasonal campaigning in Ireland continued on until the Irish military collapse at Kinsale in the winter of 1602. However, there were also permanent settlements of Redshanks in Ireland. They settled in large numbers in north County Antrim and in County Donegal. This book will present a short history of the Redshanks that settled in the Portlough precinct of the Laggan district in east Donegal.

Irish histories dealing with Ulster generally emphasize the temporary nature of the Redshanks in Ireland and the subject of the Redshanks settlements remains an understudied aspect of Ulster history. The Redshank colony in north Antrim is certainly better known, because of their links to Clann Eóin Mhóir. Around 1400, Eóin Mac Dónaill, married the daughter and heiress of Aodh Biséd of the Glens of Antrim. Through this marriage Clann Eóin Mhóir gained control of the Glens and this initiated a steady migration of Scottish Gaels into north Antrim. By the mid 1500s Clann Eóin Mhóir had expanded their territory to include the Route district west of the Glens and even more Redshanks took up residence in north Antrim. The Highland Scots came in such numbers that they changed the character of society in north Antrim and the language and culture took on a Scottish Gaelic flavour which is still evident today.

In the mid 1500s the sea traffic across the North Channel from Argyll to Ulster increased and the pace of Redshank migration to Ulster did as well. The movement of Redshanks into east Donegal took place during this time of increased military activity in Ulster. The increased demand for Redshanks in Ulster was due to Tudor English attempts to subdue the Irish lords there and Irish clan rivalries. Supplying the Irish lords with warriors was very profitable and the Redshank trade became a major part of the economy of Argyll. Literally thousands of Highland Gaels flocked to Ireland for profitable, if rather dangerous work.

By the 1560s the Ó Neill and Ó Dónaill clans in Counties Tyrone and Donegal were hiring more and more Redshanks and increasingly keeping numbers of them on their lands past the summer campaigning season. This was a time in which the nature of warfare was changing in Ireland and conflicts were continuing past the traditional cycle of summer campaigns. Another factor that encouraged Redshanks to settle in Ireland was climate change. The summers were getting cooler and crop failures were common in the west Highlands. Lands in Ireland were more fertile and Redshank migration to Ulster relieved over population and food shortages in Argyll.

From their base in Argyll, Clann Chaimbeul controlled the North Channel passage to Ulster during the 1500s. During this time Clann Chaimbeul was expanding their considerable influence into the Scottish Lowlands and into Ireland. The fifth Earl of Argyll, Giolla Easpuig Donn Caimbeul, controlled the supply of Redshanks across the North Channel in the mid-1500s. He had campaigned in Donegal himself as a young man leading a Redshank force on behalf of Clann Uí Dhónaill. Lord Argyll became deeply involved in Ulster affairs and orchestrated the dynastic marriages of his aunt Anna Mhic Dhónaill née Caimbeul and her daughter Fionnuala Nic Dhónaill, to powerful Irish lords in Ulster in the late summer of 1569. The marriages ushered in a period of migration of Caimbeul sponsored Redshanks into west Ulster. Many of these Redshanks settled in the Laggan district.

The Laggan district is in east Donegal and covers much of the Finn Valley, eastwards to the River Foyle, and north to Lough Swilly. It is comprised of two seventeenth-century precincts known as Portlough and Lifford. The district has fertile land well suited to agriculture and livestock. After the confiscation of Ó Dónaill territory by the Crown in 1607, Portlough precinct was allocated to Scottish undertakers by 1611. The precinct was divided into twelve parcels of 1,000 acres. Nine Scottish families became the 'Planters' of the

Portlough precinct and eight of them were Stewarts and Cunninghams. The plantation in Portlough precinct was unique however, because there was already an existing Scottish population living there, the Redshanks that had migrated there in the 1500s. The Stewart and Cunningham families incorporated these Redshanks into their plantation scheme. In time many of these Redshanks became part of the Ulster Scot settlement in the Laggan, yet they retained many elements of their traditional Gaelic culture.

2 The Redshank

It is not known when the term Redshank came into general use, but the word began to appear in published works by the mid-1500s. At that time Redshank was a Lowland Scottish term for a Gael from the 'Highlands.' Scottish writer John Jamison included the term in his *Supplement to the Etymological Dictionary of the Scottish Language* published in 1825.[1] His entry is an interesting summary of early usage of Redshank in English. Jamison includes quotes by the sixteenth-century writers Edmund Spenser, Thomas Stapleton, Raphael Holinshed, and John Elder. In the citations provided by Jamison the term Redshank is consistent in that it always refers to a Scottish Gael. As for the origins of the word Redshank there are two stories; one that the name came from the hair-out roe deer buskins (a calf high boot) commonly worn by Gaels and the other being that the name came from the Gaels going bare legged, or 'rough footed.'

The dress of Scottish Gaels in the 1500s was in general very similar to Irish Gaels. The *léine*, or linen shirt, and short

---

[1] John Jamieson, *Supplement To The Etymological Dictionary of the Scottish Language*, Vol. 2 (Edinburgh: University Press, 1825).

woollen jacket were worn in both Ireland and Scotland. The léine came down to just above the knee and in warm weather the wearer would be barelegged. But, while this mode of dress was common, various forms of trews were also in wide use. Most contemporary examples of the trews are ankle length, though there is one illustration from the 1570s drawn from life which shows a short trew, or a short pant, similar to a type that was worn in other parts of Western Europe at that time. The use of the kilt, or the *féileadh mór*, dates to the mid 1500s, and it was worn over the léine. So, during the 1500s when the term Redshank came into common use in Scotland, Ireland, and England, a Scottish Gael would have been dressed various ways, both barelegged and with trews. One consistent element of Gaelic dress was the hair out roe deer buskins, which is at least suggestive that this gave rise to the Scottish Gaels being known as Redshanks. However, by the 1570s, Holinshed wrote in his *Chronicles*:

> The wild Scots. otherwise called the Redshanks, or rough footed ScotsRedshanks. Rough footed Scots. (because they go bare footed and clad in mantels ouer their saffron shirts after the Irish maner) doo inhabit, Irish scots. Irish speech. they speake good Irish which they call Gachtlet, as they saie of one Gathelus, whereby they shew their originall to haue in times past béene fetched out of Ireland[2]

---

[2] Raphael Holinshed, *Holinshed's Chronicles*, Vol 1, (1587), 12.

Whatever the origin of the term is, its meaning for sixteenth-century speakers of English was clear and related to a bare legged habit of dress.

Raphael Holinshed's comments in the quote above give a good idea of how the Redshanks were viewed by outsiders. In Holinshed's work the word 'Irish' meant 'Gaelic' in modern usage. Calling Scottish Gaels 'Irish' was common in the 1500s. There was a need in the sixteenth century to differentiate between the 'Irish' or traditional Gaelic Scots and those Scots in the Lowlands, especially the eastern Lowlands, who spoke Lallans and had developed their own unique society. Additionally, Tudor writers often would describe Highland Scots in Ireland as Scots-Irish or Irish Scots, to give clarification when they were referring to Gaels from Scotland in Ireland and not native Irish Gaels.

The term Redshanks was used for several centuries. In the 1600s, in both the Wars of the Three Kingdoms (1639-1651) and the Williamite War (1689-1692), Scottish Highlanders from both Ulster and Scotland were commonly referred to as Redshanks in English. Redshanks, sometimes styled 'Redlegs,' was also used in the Caribbean to describe poor whites, usually of Gaelic origin, who were the descendants of Highland soldiers exiled there by Cromwell. It was also used to a certain extent to describe all poor whites of Gaelic ancestry, even Irish. In the Caribbean the term 'Beck e neck' or 'baked neck', meaning 'red-neck.' was also used to describe Redshanks. Any possible etymological connection to the Southern USA term Redneck can only be speculated upon, but it is of interest that in the American South this term referred in large part to the descendants of Gaels in Upland and rural areas. The etymology of 'Redneck' is thought to date to the 1640s and is linked to the Covenanter practice of wearing a red cloth around the neck to signify having become part of the Presbyterian covenant. It seems that a conflation between Redneck and Redshank has taken place over the centuries which explain the linking of the both terms with descendants of Ulster Scots in the Diaspora.

In the 1500s the Gaelic writers in Ireland called the Redshanks who had settled in Ulster, *Albanaigh*, which is Gaelic for 'Scots.' The term 'New Scots' was also used to describe Redshanks as a way to distinguish them from the 'Old Scots' who were the Gallóglaigh. The Gallóglaigh Scots settled in Ireland circa 1250 AD to 1350 AD and as previously noted, Redshank settlements came later, from 1400 to 1600 AD. By the 1600s Irish Gaelic writers changed their nomenclature and began to call Protestant Lowland Scots 'Albanaigh' and used the medieval term for a Norwegian Viking, *Fionnghall* (fair foreigner), to describe Highland Scots in their poetry of that time.[3]

Some consider Redshank as a pejorative term, but Scottish Gaelic writers in the past would describe themselves as a Redshank without any negative connotation when writing in English. Redshank is still occasionally used to describe people of Highland Scottish ancestry both in Ireland and Scotland.

---

[3] Wilson McLeod, *Divided Gaels, Gaelic Cultural Identities in Scotland and Ireland c.1200-c.1650* (Oxford: Oxford University Press 2004), 128, 129.

3 Migration to Ireland

Redshanks were a common feature of Irish armies throughout the 1500s. Almost all of them came from the western Highlands, primarily Argyll, and from the Hebridean Islands, but there are examples of Redshanks, or mercenaries, serving alongside Redshanks, coming from Ayrshire and Gallowayshire in the west Scottish Lowlands. In the 1500s the southwest Lowlands still had a sizeable Gaelic speaking population and a culture that was not significantly different from the Highlands. Clann Chaimbeul was the largest suppliers of Redshanks and this clan had lands and alliances in the western Lowlands. The Caimbeuls drew men and captains from their Lowland allies to serve in their military forces. The Redshanks were also in high demand in both the English Tudor army as well as with various armies on the Continent. As mercenaries they were considered hardier than English soldiers and superior to Irish soldiers.

The Elizabethan English were very cognizant of the Redshanks in Ireland. The *Calendar of the State Papers Relating To Ireland* has many letters and reports of English officials in Ulster concerning Redshank activities from the mid 1500s until the early 1600s. English concern and fear of the

Redshanks grew greatly when they began to settle in Ulster. By the mid-1500s the nature of the Redshanks' function was changing in Irish society. Initially, the Redshanks were only paid for time in service and there was the added benefit that the Irish lords did not need to grant them land to live on. This made them popular with these lords as they were less expensive than Gallóglaigh. However, more Scottish warriors were needed as the wars against the Elizabethan English escalated. The Redshanks were available in much larger numbers than the Gallóglaigh and the broadening scope and changing nature of warfare of the 1500s led some Irish lords, those who could afford it, to have Redshanks settle in strategic areas on their lands.

From the early fourteenth century, the Gallóglaigh were the elite element in Irish armies. They were the armoured heavy infantry and were a warrior caste that functioned much like the samurai did in medieval Japan. The Gallóglaigh were drawn from Hebridean and west Highland kindred groups. Their leaders married into the Irish aristocracy and were granted lands throughout Ireland. These warriors had not changed their basic mode of warfare and equipment of battle since the 1200s. They had an iconic dress and weapons which included a conical helmet, coat of mail, and two handed axe. Their accoutrement of war was archaic even in their heyday and was legacy of their mixed Gaelic and Norse heritage. The Gallóglaigh were very effective on the field of battle. They could stand up to the shock of English cavalry and were superior to English infantry. Every Irish lord of any importance had them in his retinue. In the 1500s however, the technology of war was changing along with the growing scale of warfare. Gallóglaigh were expensive to equip and train and it was very hard to organize them in numbers sufficient to counter the increasing English threat in Ulster. The Redshanks were available in large numbers and became the most effective way to counter the English threat.

The Redshanks were successful soldiers and had distinct advantages over the English soldiers they faced and also over the Irish infantry and Gallóglaigh. The Redshanks were hardy, living on diets which included copious amounts of oats and beef. They were impressive broad shouldered men, extremely healthy, used to cold, and able to provide for themselves in the field. They thrived in weather and conditions that would decimate English troops. The Redshanks were not a structured entity in Gaelic society as were the Gallóglaigh. The Gallóglaigh required very formal elaborate training and their sons would often follow their fathers into the profession. In this sense the Gallóglaigh were a bona fide warrior caste and were more than simple mercenaries. The Redshanks were much more flexible. There were some similarities of course and at times there was very little difference between a Redshank warrior and a Gallóglach. The Redshanks were also soldiers for hire and they came from the same Hebridean and Argyll kinships as did the original Gallóglaigh. The Redshanks were trained soldiers, but they were not a Gaelic societal institution as were the Gallóglaigh. As soldiers they were straight forward mercenaries, but they would farm, or fish, or turn to a trade if they tired of a soldier's life.

The Redshanks were also more flexible even as warriors. They were quick to take up the use of firearms to supplement their two handed swords and bows and they were noted for their excellent marksmanship. They provided the swiftness of Gaelic light infantry, or the *Ceithearn*, yet also had the dynamic hitting power and shock of the Gallóglaigh. By 1575 Redshank pay was equal to that of the famed Gallóglaigh.[4] An example of their increasing importance in Ireland is found in the 1566 letter to the Elizabethan court by Sir Francis Knollys, an English agent in Ireland. The letter referenced the growing number of Redshanks the English encountered in the Irish armies they faced. Knollys reported to Queen Elizabeth that 300 Redshanks were 'harder to be vanquished in battle than 600 Irishmen.'[5]

As mentioned, the initial settlement of Redshanks in Ulster was in the Glens of north Antrim. The Biséd family of Scotland had gained control of the Glens circa 1245 AD. The family held the Glens until the end of the 1300s when the head of the clan, Eóin Mac Eóin, failed to produce a male heir. His oldest daughter, Máire Nic Eóin, married Eóin Mór Mac Dónaill of Clann Eóin Mhóir in 1399 AD. The marriage was the beginning of a large migration of Redshanks into north Antrim under Clann Dhónaill's auspices. These Redshanks settled in the Glens and Route districts that were controlled by Clann Dhónaill. In 1542 John Travers, the Master of the Ordnance in Ireland wrote:

> where as a company of Irishe Scottes
> otherwise called Redshankes daily commeth
> into the northe parties of Irelande and
> purchaseth castels and piles uppon the

---

[4] Ian Heath, *The Irish Wars 1485-1603* (London: Osprey Publishing, 1993), 11.
[5] Hans Claude Hamilton, ed., *Calendar of the State Papers Relating to Ireland* (London: Longman, Green, Longman & Roberts, 1860), 302.

seecoste there so as it is thought that there be at this present above the nombre of 2 or 3 thousande of them within this Realme...[6]

In April of 1571 Lord Justice William FitzWilliam wrote to the Privy Council:

The Scots in the North build, manure the ground, and settle, as though they should never be removed.[7]

There is a description of Redshanks found in the early 1600s book *Beatha Aodha Ruaidh Uí Dhomhnaill* (Life of Aodh Rua Ó Dónaill), written by the seanchaí (historian) of Clann Uí Dhónaill, Lughaidh Ó Cléirigh:

They were recognized among the Irish soldier by the distinction of their arms and clothing, their habits and language, for their exterior dress was mottled cloaks of many colours with a fringe to their shins and claves, their belts were over their loins outside their cloaks. Many of them had swords with hafts of horn, large and warlike, over their shoulders. It was necessary for the soldier to grip the very haft of his sword with both hands when he would strike a blow with it. Others of them had bows of carved woods strong for use, with well seasoned strings of

---

[6] Hamilton, *Calendar*, 302.
[7] Ibid., 444.

hemp, and arrows sharp pointed, whizzing in flight.[8]

Ó Cléirigh's comments referred to an arrival in Derry of a thousand Scottish Gaels led by Dónall Gorm Mac Dónaill (presumably from Skye) and a Mac Leóid of Arran in 1594. These Redshanks were in the service of Aodh Rua Ó Dónaill.

Ó Cléirigh was an eye witness of the Redshanks living in west Ulster and his comments provide an accurate assessment of their dress, weapons and characteristics. By the late 1500s the unique Scottish dress of the belted kilt was worn by many Redshanks. The two handed swords and bows described by Ó Cléirigh were favourite weapons of the Redshanks. Ó Cléirigh also notes the Gaelic dialect of the Redshanks, which was unique to the Isles and Argyll. As in Antrim, so many Redshanks settled in west Ulster that they influenced the Gaelic spoken there, giving it many elements of Scottish Gaelic.

The Redshank migration to Antrim came primarily from the Hebrides and Kintyre, which were lands controlled by Clann Eóin Mhóir. The Redshank movement into West Ulster came primarily from mid Argyll and western Lennox and was organized by Clann Chaimbeul.

---

[8] Lughaidh Ó Cléirigh, *Beatha Aodha Ruaidh Uí Dhómhnaill*, trans. Paul Walsh (Cork: University College, 2012. http://www.ucc.ie/celt.

4 Clann Chaimbeul

Clann Chaimbeul was the catalyst for the migration of Redshanks into the Laggan district of Donegal. This powerful clan extended their influence into Ulster in the 1500s and had a profound effect on Ulster and even Irish history. The chief of Clann Chaimbeul in the mid 1500s was the fifth Earl of Argyll, Giolla Easpuig Donn Caimbeul. It was his plans that were ultimately responsible for the movement of Redshanks from Argyll to east Donegal. His first cousin was Fionnuala Níc Dhónaill (Iníon Dubh) and it was on her lands in the Laggan that the majority of the Caimbeul sponsored Redshanks settled.

Clann Chaimbeul in the 1500s was the most dynamic Gaelic family in Scotland. They recognised the changing world of the early modern period and adjusted to it. Their chiefs were the Earls of Argyll and they provided excellent leadership for their tribe. Clann Chaimbeul were old order traditional Gaels in every sense, but they operated and had ambitions outside the Gaelic world. Under the leadership of the Earls of Argyll the clan established cadet families in the Scottish Lowlands and they had a presence in the Scottish Court in Edinburgh. The sons of the clan's gentry received formal training in the Gaelic tradition, but also went to universities in the Lowlands. The Earls established trading houses in Scotland and England. The members of the Earls' court were tri-lingual and could communicate in their native Gaelic, as well as Lallans and Latin. The Earls patronised the Gaelic arts. There were the great poets, men of letters, and musicians, from Ireland and the Scottish Gaeltacht at the Earls' court and yet at the same time Lowland artisans and craftsmen were also in residence there. The Earls were patrons of Bishop John Carswell, known in Argyll as Seon Carsuel. In 1567, with Caimbeul patronage, he produced a translation of the *Book of Common Order*, or *Foirm na nUrrnuidheadh*, which was the first book printed in the Gaelic language. The House of Caimbeul was a powerful force in the Gaelic world and beyond and in the mid 1500s they turned their considerable influence toward Ulster.

The fifth Earl of Argyll was born in 1538 and was earl from 1558 until his death in 1573. Argyll's accomplishments were many despite his premature death by illness. He held court at Inverary Castle in mid Argyll near the shores of Loch Fyne. Lord Argyll was a principal player in many of the major events of his day in both Ireland and Scotland. He was an interesting man in many regards. He was a Protestant and an enthusiastic patron of the Reformed faith in the Scottish Gaeltacht, yet he also supported the Roman Catholic Mary Queen of Scots and had no qualms about having Irish and Scottish Catholic lords as allies. Lord Argyll was blessed with a large dose of Caimbeul pragmatism. A very profitable part of his family business was that of broker and supplier of Redshanks to the Irish lords in Ulster. In the mid 1500s the use of Redshank mercenaries by the Irish chiefs in Ulster grew greatly. Not only were the Redshanks a very profitable business for Lord Argyll, but they also allowed him to promote his political agenda in Scotland and Ireland.

In 1555 Clann Chaimbeul extended their sphere of influence and operations into Ireland. In Donegal that year a bitter Ó Dónaill power struggle erupted between Calbhach Ó Dónaill and his father Manus Ó Dónaill. Calbhach Ó Dónaill travelled to Argyll to meet with the fourth Earl of Argyll to negotiate for Caimbeul Redshanks and military expertise. The fourth Earl allowed his son, the young Giolla Easpuig Donn to lead the expedition. This gave Giolla Easpuig Donn first hand military experience in Ulster. The campaign was a total success and Giolla Easpuig Donn established a long term friendship with Calbhach Ó Dónaill. This friendship and his experience in Ulster would prove important to the future fifth Earl.

The details of how the Caimbeuls were drawn into Ulster affairs reads like a sordid soap opera plot albeit much more complex. In 1558 the fourth Earl of Argyll died and his son Giolla Easpuig Donn became the fifth Earl. His father left a pretty, young widow, Giolla Easpuig Donn's stepmother. This stepmother was a powerful woman in her own right. She was Catriona Nic Ghiolla Eáin, the daughter of Eachann Mór Mac Giolla Eáin who was taoiseach of Clann Mhic Ghiolla Eáin on Mull. Her clan was both allies of Clann Chaimbeul and a source of Redshanks. The Lord Argyll had to find a suitable new husband for his stepmother and he had just the man, his friend Calbhach Ó Dónaill, the new taoiseach of the Ó Dónaills. Catriona arrived in Donegal with 2,000 Redshanks accompanying her and in 1560 she and Calbhach were wed. The Earl had killed two birds with one stone with the marriage. He reaped considerable profit of 100 pounds sterling per annum for Redshanks provided to Calbhach and joined his house to the Ó Dónaill clan. The marriage also drew the Earl much deeper into Ulster politics.

The late 1560s were very busy in Ulster. There were clan conflicts and the Elizabethan English were constantly testing the Gaelic defences in Ulster. Things went well for Calbhach at first. In 1561 Calbhach was cooperating with the Elizabethan English in order to strengthen his hold upon his clan. He resigned his lands to the Crown, a formality, as they were then 'given' to him by Elizabeth I and he was proclaimed the Earl of Tír Chónaill. At this time, Seaán Ó Neill, who commanded the strongest military force in Ulster, demanded fealty from all the clans in Ulster, including his great rivals, Clann Uí Dhónaill. Calbhach received intelligence that Seaán had entered Tír Chónaill to demand Calbhach's fealty. Calbhach, however, launched a surprise night raid on Seaán's camp killing and capturing many of Seaán's men and sending the rest fleeing into the night, including Seaán himself. This embarrassing defeat did not sit well with Seaán and he managed to enact his revenge later in the year by surprising Calbhach and his wife while they were staying at a monastery in Tír Chónaill. Seaán surrounded the monastery and took both Calbhach and Catriona prisoner.

After the capture there were rumours that Catriona had become Seaán's sex slave or perhaps mistress. The version of the story that reached Lord Argyll was she was in chains and Seaán was having his way with her often. Lord Argyll considered a rescue attempt of his stepmother, but matters in Scotland kept him occupied and he turned the problem over to the Elizabethan English officials in Ireland, who did absolutely nothing. Losing his patience, Lord Argyll then offered a ransom of 300 pounds sterling and 400 Redshanks. This generous ransom was accepted by Seaán who then freed Calbhach Ó Dónaill, however, Catriona chose to remain with Seaán, raising more than a few Gaelic eyebrows. She went on to marry Seaán in 1565 and bore him several sons.

That was not the end of sexual politics in this tale however, as even more interesting events loomed ahead. Calbhach plotted his revenge, but years of harsh treatment in Seaán's dungeon had taken its toll, and he passed away in 1566. His half-brother, Aodh Mac Manus Ó Dónaill was then inaugurated as 'The Ó Dónaill.' To follow this course of events, it is necessary to go to the previous year when Seaán went to war against his other clan rivals, Clann Dhónaill of north Antrim. Clann Dhónaill was a pan Gaelic one and held lands in northern Ireland and Scotland. In May of 1565 Seaán defeated them in the battle of Glentaisie. Seaán captured the overall chief of the clan, Seamus Mac Dónaill, along with his brother, Somhairle Buí Mac Dónaill, who was the head of the north Antrim branch of the clan. Seamus was married to Anna Caimbeul who was the aunt of Lord Argyll. Seamus Mac Dónaill was wounded in the battle and later died of his wounds in July of 1565 while in Seaán's dungeon. The death of Anna Caimbeul's husband at Seaán's hands brought Lord Argyll into the matter.

Caimbeul women were important assets to their clan. They married important people for important reasons. Anna Caimbeul was the daughter of Cailean Caimbeul, the third Earl of Argyll. Her first marriage to James Stewart of Bute ended in annulment. Her second marriage was to Seamus Mac Dónaill the chief of Clann Dhónaill. They had a very successful marriage producing many children and the Mac Dónaill and Caimbeul Houses were allied at this time. The death of Anna's husband by Seaán in 1565 brought great instability to Ulster. Anna Caimbeul was very close to her nephew, the fifth Earl of Argyll, and he made plans to protect her and her children and to free Seamus Mac Dónaill's brother, Somhairle Buí Mac Dónaill, from Seaán. This complex situation did partially resolve itself in the spring of 1567.

Seaán Ó Neill once again invaded Donegal, however this time he was utterly defeated at the battle of Farsetmore, just north of Letterkenny, on 8 May 1567. It was a large clan battle between Clann Uí Dhónaill under Aodh Mac Manus Ó Dónaill and Clann Uí Neill under Seaán Ó Neill. Each side had around 2,000 men, comprised of Irish warriors, Gallóglaigh, and Redshanks. Seaán's army was routed with very high casualties. He did manage to retreat back across the Foyle River. Seaán needed troops and needed them fast in case the Ó Dónaills followed up on their victory. He was desperate and decided to parley with Clann Dhónaill. He wanted to make peace with them and use their Redshanks to defend his home territory.

Seaán made overtures that he was willing to send Catriona back to her father and marry Anna Caimbeul, the widow of Seamus Mac Dónaill. Now the problem with this plan was obvious. Seaán had killed Anna Caimbeul's husband and she would have preferred his head on a platter to marriage. Nevertheless, Seaán rode to north Antrim with only his personal bodyguard, taking with him Somhairle Buí Mac

Dónaill, who was still his prisoner. He began negotiations with Alasdair Óg Mac Dónaill, the acting head of Clann Dhónaill and brother of Seamus and Somhairle Buí Mac Dónaill. Seaán met with Alasdair Óg at Cushendun, in the Glens of Antrim on 31 May 1567. Alasdair Óg was there with a body of Redshanks and some of them had been recruited for him by Anna's nephew, Lord Argyll. The negotiations would have been difficult for Seaán as he was in a very vulnerable position after the near destruction of his army at Farsetmore, plus Somhairle Buí once in Cushendun was now a free man. This weakness would cost Seaán everything.

The death of Seaán Ó Neill came on 2 June 1567. The facts are as follows: Alasdair Óg Mac Dónaill, along with the captain of his Redshanks, and a few chosen warriors, walked into a room to 'negotiate' with Seaán. When they left the room the great Irish chief was dead. The exact details of his death will never be known, but there were several parties that certainly wanted him dead. The Mac Dónaills wanted revenge and Lord Argyll had plans in Ulster that would benefit from Seaán's removal from the scene. The Elizabethan English also would benefit from Seaán's death. The English circulated a story that Seaán died in a drunken brawl, but the truth was he was killed on the third day of his negotiations with Alasdair Óg. It is very possible the English were the instigators of the killing, as one of their agents was close enough to the event to claim Seaán's head several days later, which he took back to Dublin to present to the English government there. With Seaán's death there was a great power vacuum in Ulster and it would not go unfilled.

The death of Seaán solved one problem for Lord Argyll and presented him with a great opportunity to extend his influence into Ulster. He had a plan for a great Ulster alliance between the clans Caimbeul, Ó Dónaill, Ó Neill, and Mac Dónaill. Lord Argyll once again turned to the women of his clan. He proposed that his Aunt, Anna Mhic Dhónaill née Caimbeul, the widow of Seamus Mac Dónaill, marry the successor to Seaán, who was Tarlach Luineach Ó Neill, and furthermore, that Anna's daughter, Fionnuala Nic Dhónaill, marry the head of the Ó Dónaill clan, Aodh Mac Manus Ó Dónaill. It was bold, it was genius, and it worked. All parties agreed and the marriages were set to take place in the summer of 1568. However, matters in Scotland relating to Lord Argyll's support of Mary Queen of Scots became critical and the marriages were put on hold.

In Scotland Lord Argyll's affairs were also incredibly complex as he was in the very middle of the tumultuous events surrounding Mary Queen of Scots' attempt to hold onto power. Lord Argyll was a Protestant and a great supporter of that faith in Argyll. He was at times in open rebellion against the Catholic Queen, yet in the end he became her friend and ally. Lord Argyll eventually became the Queen's trusted advisor and military commander and as the drama of Mary's life played out in 1567, he was drawn into the dramatic end of her reign as queen of Scotland. On 13 May 1568 Lord Argyll led the army in support of Mary Queen of Scots at the battle of Langside. His behaviour during the affair is still an intriguing mystery. He withdrew his troops just prior to the battle of Langside, claiming he had suffered an epileptic fit though many of his peers did not believe him. Mary's army became demoralised and many of her soldiers deserted prior to the battle. Whatever the case, Lord Argyll was unable or chose not to be on the field that day and his military skills and Redshanks were desperately needed. The battle was a disaster for Mary. Lord Argyll's absence also prevented him from taking Mary to a place of safety in Scotland. She made a very unwise decision to flee to England. Lord Argyll then returned to Inverary castle and turned his full attention back to Ulster. The weddings of Anna Mhic Dhónail and her daughter Fionnuala Nic Dhónaill were rescheduled for the late summer of 1569.

The English tried to prevent the weddings of Anna and Fionnuala from taking place. The mere suggestion of the great Gaelic clans of the north, Ó Neill, Ó Dónaill, Mac Dónaill, and Caimbeul, working in unison, was their worst nightmare come true. There was very little the English could do to prevent the event however, because Lord Argyll's fleet dominated the North Channel between Scotland and Ulster. Fitzwilliam, the English governor in Ireland, warned that Tarlach Ó Neill and Aodh Mac Manus Ó Dónaill wanted Scottish wives in order 'to breed a new sort of rebel out of their loins.'[9] With great preparation the joint weddings took place in late summer of 1569 on the island of Rathlin off the north Antrim coast. Anna and her daughter Fionnuala left Argyll for Islay and from there journeyed south to Rathlin Island. Their party included 32 galleys and around 4,000 Redshanks. The wedding celebration lasted for two full weeks and the gentry of the northern Gaelic world were all in attendance. The marriages would change the course of Irish history.

---

[9] Jane E A Dawson, *The Politics of Religion in the Age of Mary Queen of Scots, The Earl of Argyll and the Struggle for Britain and Ireland* (Cambridge: Cambridge University Press, 2002), 162.

Anna and her daughter Fionnuala played a leading role in Irish resistance to English rule in the latter half of the 1500s. They were responsible for raising Scottish support of the Irish lords they had married. They were well suited to the task. They were Gaelic nobility, highly educated, multi-lingual and had experience in both the traditional Gaelic and the emerging British world. Both women were immensely powerful because they controlled the flow of Redshanks into Ulster through their Caimbeul connections. Both women also had married older men and as their husbands aged the women became very influential in their husbands' clans. Anna and Fionnuala brought thousands of Caimbeul Redshanks to Ireland from 1569 to 1600 as the Tudor English put pressure upon the great Irish lords of the north. Fionnuala is better known in Irish history as Iníon Dubh (black haired daughter) and it was her support of the Ó Dónaill clan in Donegal that brought Redshanks into the Laggan district.

5 Iníon Dubh

The River Foyle is a large, brown water, tidal river, that flows north into Loch Foyle and then on into the Atlantic Ocean and is known for being one of the best salmon fishing areas in Ireland. The river begins at the town of Lifford from the confluence of the Finn and Mourne rivers. The low lands on the west side of the river are called the Laggan district taking that name from the Gaelic word *lagan*, meaning a hollow or low lying area. In the Laggan is the small market town of St Johnston. The lands around St Johnston are green and fertile and there you will see the many shades of Irish green. It is a beautiful area where farms still flourish and time is marked by the changing seasons. It was in the St Johnston area that Iníon Dubh settled after her marriage to Aodh Mac Manus Ó Dónaill in late summer of 1569.

Iníon Dubh and her Redshanks settled in the part of the Laggan that was called the Portlough precinct in Elizabethan times. The Portlough precinct was an administrative district that corresponds to Taughboyne, All Saints, Raymoghy, and part of Raphoe parishes today. Portlough precinct was the heart of the Laggan district and it included the important Foyle River ports that were used by the Redshanks to land their west

Highland birlinns, which were the unique and nimble galleys used by Gaels.

The Laggan was the richest and most productive land of the Clann Uí Dhónaill and it also had a navigable river by which both enemy and friend could travel deep into Ó Dónaill territory. A large number of Caimbeul Redshanks accompanied Iníon Dubh to her new home and settled there to protect this vital part of Ó Dónaill territory. Accounts vary, but the number of Redshanks that accompanied her initially was around 1,000. There was throughout her time in the Laggan an ebb and flow of Redshanks dictated by the military needs Clann Uí Dhónaill. Iníon Dubh and her mother were aggressive in their efforts to preserve Ulster from English rule and their weapon of choice were the tall, fair, broad shouldered Gaels of Argyll and southern Hebrides. Iníon Dubh became one of the most important people in Ireland in the late 1500s, because of the large number of formidable Redshanks at her command.

Iníon Dubh was a Scottish Gaelic aristocrat, a high born Gael, and possessed remarkable qualities. As a teenager she was part of the Scottish court in Edinburgh. Her father had been the head of Clann Dhónaill, her mother the daughter of the head of Clann Chaimbeul, and she became a heroine of the Irish in the north. She was at home in traditional Gaelic society and yet more than able to interact with the Elizabethan English and Lowland Scots on their terms. She is remembered best for her heroic defence of her sons. Her sons had glorious but tragic lives as Gaelic warriors. Her oldest son, Aodh Rua Ó Dónaill, along with Aodh Mór Ó Neill, had many victories against the English and very nearly drove the English out of Ireland in the Nine Years' War (1594-1603).

Lughaidh Ó Cléirigh, a contemporary of Iníon Dubh, and biographer of her son, Aodh Rua, wrote of her, '... she was the head of advice and counsel of the Ceníl Conaill (Clann Uí Dhónaill), and though she was calm and very deliberate and much praised for her womanly qualities, she had the heart of a hero and mind of soldier.'[10] To these admirable traits she also commanded a force of Redshanks from Argyll and she was not afraid to put them into use.

Iníon Dubh's main residence in the Laggan was the castle at Mongavlin, just south of St Johnston. She had a secondary house at Carrigans, just north of St Johnston. These locations were not random; both were river harbours where the Redshank galleys could easily land. It is not a large area. Carrigans is only one and three quarters mile north of St Johnston and Mongavlin is only two and a quarter miles to its south. Many of Iníon Dubh's Redshanks settled around her within the five or so miles between Mongavlin and Carrigans. The settlement of so many Scottish Gaels had the desired effect and this strategic district became a no-go area for English and hostile Irish both.

By the mid-1500s Redshanks were settling in Ulster and not returning back to Argyll or the Hebrides. The Redshanks with Iníon Dubh were a continuation of this new migration, but specifically into east Donegal. By 1580 Iníon Dubh and her Redshanks began to dominate the political and military affairs of western Ulster. She was by this time the de

---

[10] Lughaidh Ó Cléirigh, 39.

facto head of Clann Uí Dhónaill. Her husband's poor health and loss of mental clarity forced her into a position of leadership within Clann Uí Dhónaill. She was up to the task. Her early life in the Scottish court and her links to Clann Chaimbeul and Clann Dhónaill gave her the needed upbringing, kinship connections, and experience. Perhaps most important was Iníon Dubh had her own army, which she paid and commanded personally. Her Redshanks were completely devoted to her and this made her the most powerful person in west Ulster. It is worth mentioning that she also had an iron will.

There were many threats to Iníon Dubh and her family. The children of her husband by his first wife were rivals to her own children and there was always the English to contend with. The explosive mixture of clan dynastic rivalries and English Machiavellian politics were brutal and tragic to Iníon Dubh and her children.

In 1587 John Perrot, the English Lord Deputy of Ireland, wanted hostages from the Ó Dónaills to insure that they would not aid the Spanish in their war against England. He plotted to kidnap Iníon Dubh and her husband Aodh Mac Manus, but only their oldest son Aodh Rua fell into English hands. He was imprisoned in Dublin Castle. Iníon Dubh threw all her energies into freeing her son and making him the head of Clann Uí Dhónaill. In 1588 Iníon Dubh attempted to obtain the release of Aodh Rua by rounding up some Spanish Armada survivors that had made land fall in Donegal and presenting them to the English in Dublin as an exchange for her son. The English took the prisoners, but had them all executed and kept Aodh Rua in his dungeon cell. She then told the English she would work with the Spanish if they did not release him, again she had no success.

It was decidedly unhealthy to cross Iníon Dubh in matters relating to her children. She was in a very vulnerable position with her husband in failing health and her oldest son a prisoner of the English, yet she managed to hold on to power by virtue of her Redshanks. By the late 1580s some within Clann Uí Dhónaill considered Aodh Mac Manus unfit to be head of the clan. The first rival to press the issue was Aodh Mac Calbhach Ó Gallchobhair. He was a somewhat mysterious figure, perhaps an illegitimate son of Calbhach Ó Dónaill, or perhaps fostered with Calbhach's family. Whatever the case, he let it be known he could take the headship of the clan. Aodh Mac Calbhach had cooperated with the English and had been a factor in the infamous murder of Iníon Dubh's first cousin, Alasdair Mac Somhairle Mhic Dhónaill. In 1588 Aodh Mac Calbhach attempted to visit Iníon Dubh at her castle south of St Johnston and press the issue. He felt he was in a position to seize power since Aodh Rua was in a Dublin dungeon and Aodh Mac Manus unfit to rule. Iníon Dubh was not impressed. She addressed her beloved Redshanks about the need for justice and revenge upon Aodh Mac Calbhach. They fulfilled that need by attacking Aodh Mac Calbhach and his party and killing them all.

Another of her chief rivals was her husband's son by an earlier marriage, Dónall Mac Aodh Ó Dónaill. Again, with Aodh Mac Manus in poor health and Aodh Rua still in captivity, Dónall proclaimed himself as head of Clann Uí Dhónaill. He also severely underestimated Iníon Dubh. Iníon

Dubh took command of her army of Redshanks and marched out to meet Dónall Ó Dónaill in battle. Dónall assembled a formidable host that included his factions within Clann Uí Dhónaill, along with Clann Mhic Suibhne of Banagh, Clann Mhic Suibhne of Munster, and Clann Uí Bhaoighill. The Battle of Derrylaghan took place on 14 September 1590, when the two armies met to the south of Gleann Cholm Cille, near the village of Teileann. The Redshanks used their bows to stun Dónall's army and then closed with their two handed swords. Dónall's army was crushed and he was killed along with many of the Irish nobles that supported him and 200 of their men.

Aodh Rua finally escaped Dublin Castle in December of 1592. Iníon Dubh persuaded her husband to abdicate and Aodh Rua became The Ó Dónaill. Iníon Dubh bought off the last rival claiming the headship of the clan, Niall Garbh Ó Dónaill, and arranged a marriage between him and her daughter Nuala. From that point on, the history of Aodh Rua is the history of Ireland. He allied himself with Aodh Mór Ó Neill and that began the Nine Years War. The two great clans, which in the past had so often been at war with each other, now joined to fight a common enemy, the English. In the conflict Aodh Rua had many victories and defeated every English army sent to destroy him for several years. The Laggan Redshanks were the heart of his army. Aodh Rua had military success in Ulster, where he could use the terrain to his advantage and his army was well supplied and had the support of the people. The war grew in scope however and he took his army south to Cork to assist a Spanish force which had landed there. In January of 1602 the end came with the pivotal battle of Kinsale and the utter defeat of Aodh Rua and his ally Aodh Mór Ó Neill, by Lord Mountjoy and his well-trained English army. Aodh Rua took a ship to Spain to organize further resistance, but he died in September of 1602, very possibly poisoned by an English agent.

His friend and ally, Aodh Mór Ó Neill, returned to Ulster after the defeat at Kinsale. In 1607 he too left for Spain, along with Aodh Rua's brother, Ruairí, who had become The Ó Dónaill after his brother's death. This is called the Flight of the Earls. Their intention was to raise money and an army to continue the war. They set sail from Rathmullan, a small village on the shore of Loch Swilly, in County Donegal, with ninety followers, many of these the cream of Ulster's Gaelic nobles. Their destination was Spain, but they landed first in France where some made their way to Spanish Flanders, while others continued on to Rome. Their plans came ultimately to nothing and both Ruairí Ó Dónaill and Aodh Mór Ó Neill died in exile.

By 1608 all of Iníon Dubh's male children were dead. One of her last recorded acts was a small piece of unfinished business. Niall Garbh Ó Dónaill had turned traitor in the end, supporting the English against Aodh Rua. Iníon Dubh implicated Niall Garbh in a failed uprising in 1608 and he spent the rest of his days in the Tower in London where he died. Iníon Dubh's daughter, Nuala left Niall Garbh, taking their children with her. Iníon Dubh then retired to the small village of Kilmacrennan, west of Letterkenny, to live out her life in relative peace and quiet.

The year of 1609 brought great change in Ulster. The old Gaelic order had finally been broken and this allowed for the Plantation of Ulster. The lands of Clann Uí Dhónaill were confiscated under James I. This included Iníon Dubh's lands in the Laggan around St Johnston which were located in the Portlough precinct. The Portlough precinct was planted by Scots and the two main families granted this choice land were the Stewarts and Cunninghams. Both families had close ties to James I and received almost the entire precinct with instructions to plant it with 'civil' Scots. However, there was already a Scottish community on the land. Iníon Dubh's Caimbeul Redshanks were still living in the Portlough precinct.

6 Portlough Precinct

By 1609 the Redshanks of Portlough precinct were no longer employed by Iníon Dubh and their ties to Clann Uí Dhónaill were a thing of the past. There was a new order that would decide their fate. Among this new order were Scottish lords that took the Ó Dónaill lands in Portlough precinct. Like the Ó Dónaill chiefs before them the Scottish lords also valued the Redshanks for their martial abilities. Even before the Gaelic military collapse after Kinsale in the winter of 1602 the Redshank community on the Foyle was seen as a possible asset to British, and specifically to Scottish, interests in Ulster. This was during the end phase of the Nine Year's War at a time when the Elizabethan English were hard pressed in Ulster. Plans were proposed to hire the Foyle Redshanks by pro-British factions.

It was a bold idea since those very Redshanks had defeated English armies on the field of battle many times. The Redshank soldiers were the crucial military element that kept Ulster free of English domination in the 1500s. There was naturally a concern about the loyalties of the Foyle Redshanks, but there were mitigating factors, including the Foyle Redshanks' Scottish clan ties and links to important Scottish families, such as the Caimbeuls of Argyll and Hamiltons of Arran.

These clan connections and family ties were important in the Scottish world. Iníon Dubh's mother, Anna Caimbeul, was the daughter of the third Earl of Argyll. Her first cousins were the fourth and fifth Earls of Argyll. The mother of the fifth Earl of Argyll was Helen Hamilton, the eldest daughter of the first Earl of Arran, James Hamilton. Most of the Foyle Redshanks were from the Caimbeul lands in mid Argyll or from the lands of their allies in the Lennox district of Scotland. These Redshanks had a degree of loyalty to Caimbeul interests in the Ulster. Iníon Dubh, her mother, the Earls of Argyll, the Hamiltons of Arran, the Stewarts of Lennox, were all part of an elaborate kinship group through which mutual policies and ambitions were implemented and the Redshanks became a tool to implement their plans.

By the late 1500s the Caimbeuls and Hamiltons were political and military allies, in-laws, and were involved in affairs in both Scotland and Ireland. Both families had a presence in the Scottish royal court and the ear of James VI of Scotland who became James I of England, and was the monarch that initiated the Plantation of Ulster. For the Redshanks the transition from a life serving Iníon Dubh to a life dominated by the Scottish lords that took over her lands was not as traumatic as it might appear. The Stewarts of Lennox in Portlough precinct were also kinsmen to Iníon Dubh through her maternal Caimbeul family. Within this paradigm the Foyle Redshanks became part of Scottish ambitions in the region.

In the *Calendar of the State Papers Relating To Ireland, Of The Reign of Elizabeth*, there is correspondence promoting the use of the Foyle Redshanks. The idea of using Scottish mercenaries was not new to the British. Henry VIII used Gaelic light infantry, called Ceithearn, in his armies. The English even hired a few Gallóglaigh companies. The Redshanks living along the Foyle could be a great asset in sustaining British interest in west Ulster, if they could be persuaded to serve.

In November of 1600 the English Privy Council wrote to Henry Docwra, the English Commander in the River Foyle area, suggesting the use of Redshanks. In the end the plan was not carried out, because the Irish defeat at Kinsale ended the need for the Redshanks. However, the idea of using the Foyle Redshanks was also in the minds of several prominent Scots with ambitions in Ulster. One of these Scots was a Gael from Argyll, Donnchadh Caimbeul, who was the illegitimate son of Giolla Easpuig Donn Caimbeul and he was a kinsman to Iníon Dubh. Donnchadh Caimbeul was true to his surname. Being a son of the Argyll court, he was a traditional Gael, yet he was also part of the emerging British world. Like many other Caimbeuls, he knew how to combine both the Gaelic and British political tools at his disposal to further the interest of his family and their allies, which at that point in time was shifting from the Gaelic world to promoting the interest of James VI of Scotland.

In March of 1601 Donnchadh Caimbeul wrote to Sir Robert Cecil, the English Secretary of State, suggesting the use of certain Redshanks to further Elizabeth I's interest in Ulster. His letter is of great interest because it demonstrates how the

Foyle Redshanks were viewed by the Scottish officials that would later be part of the Plantation in east Donegal. In his letter to Cecil, Caimbeul specifies use of the 'civil Irish Scots'[11] to secure strategic areas along the Foyle River. He does not mince words in his recommendations and further clarifies which Redshanks are to be used, 'As for the civil Irish, the Campbells only are to be chosen.'[12] His use of the word 'Irish' to describe the Caimbeul Redshanks was common among the English of that period. They used Irish as a synonym for Gael and applied it to both Irish and Scottish Gaels.

Because of Donnchadh's background, family connections and experience, he believed the Caimbeul Redshanks could be counted on. Their loyalties could be assured by their Gaelic clan affiliation, and of significance, many of the Caimbeul Redshanks were Protestant. The fifth Earl of Argyll was an early convert to the Reformed faith and had vigorously set about converting the Caimbeul rank and file and their allies to his new religion. It was from this population of Gaels that Iníon Dubh's Redshanks were recruited. Donnchadh Caimbeul and Iníon Dubh were contemporaries. They would have known each other and shared a hearth fire in Inverary castle during Iníon Dubh's trips to Argyll to procure her Redshanks. Donnchadh Caimbeul was knowledgeable about the nature of these particular Redshanks.

Like many other high born Caimbeuls, Donnchadh Caimbeul obtained a good position in life, in his case, as an

---

[11] Hamilton, *Calendar*, 255, 256.

[12] Ibid 256

40

Established Church official in Ireland. To accomplish this he joined the Established Church. While it may seem odd that a man from such a strong Reformed faith family would do this, this was very normal Caimbeul behaviour. Among the Caimbeuls pragmatism was a virtue to further their clan's interests and the end justified the means. Donnchadh Caimbeul did well in the Established Church and he served as Dean of Limerick and coadjutor bishop there from 1588 to 1603.

His letter to Sir Robert Cecil also goes into details as to which Scottish families should be used in Ulster. In addition to the Caimbeul Irish Scots along the Foyle he lists the Hamiltons of Arran. This was the family of his father's mother, Helen Hamilton, and the related Abercorn Hamilton family received large tracks of land in northwest Tyrone just a few years later. The Hamiltons were also a family familiar with traditional Gaelic society as some of their lands in Scotland were in the Scottish Gaeltacht. They appreciated the Redshanks and their military usefulness.

As mentioned, the plans to hire the Foyle Redshanks never were brought to fruition since by 1603 the Nine Year's War was winding down and additional troops were not needed. The letter by Donnchadh Caimbeul however, does show how the Caimbeul Redshanks were viewed by the incoming Scottish Planters that settled in east Donegal. In March of 1603 Queen Elizabeth I died and the Scottish King James VI ascended to the united throne of England and Scotland as James I. A few months later Donnchadh Caimbeul was appointed Bishop of Raphoe in Donegal, but died before he could be consecrated. However, his idea of incorporating the

Caimbeul Redshanks to secure the Laggan did eventually happen.

Iníon Dubh remained at Mongavlin in 1608 as the Plantation was being organised in London. When the Plantation was implemented by James I, she was one of the 'native' Undertakers, or people that were given land by the Crown. On the face of it, her grant of land by the Crown would appear to be an amazing event given her long period of resistance to English encroachment into Ulster and the fact that her son very nearly drove the English out of Ireland entirely. In 1611 Iníon Dubh was given 598 acres at Kilmacrenan, west of Letterkenny, where she relocated and retired from political life. Put into the context of her position within the Caimbeul extended kinship group, which included James I, it is understandable how she managed to weather such a tumultuous storm of change.

Iníon Dubh's land in Portlough precinct went to two prominent Scottish families, the Stewarts and Cunninghams. It is very possible that the lands the Stewarts received from James I in Portlough were part of the intricate etiquette of kinship and political alliances of these prominent Scottish families. The head of this Stewart family was the Duke of Lennox, Ludovic Stewart, who was a cousin to Iníon Dubh through her maternal Caimbeul line. He was also cousin to the King James I. In 1580 the head of the House of Darnley, King James Stewart VI of Scots, who became James I, granted the title Duke of Lennox to his cousin Esmé Stewart, who was Ludovic's father. Duke Ludovic and his illegitimate son, John Stewart, obtained large portions of Iníon Dubh's land and her residence, Mongavlin Castle.

The Redshanks along the Foyle remained after Iníon Dubh's departure. It was their Caimbeul links and early exposure to the Reformed faith, along with their reputation as elite fighting men, which made them not only acceptable to the incoming Stewarts and Cunninghams, but a welcomed van guard. The opinions about the Caimbeul Redshanks expressed by Donnchadh Caimbeul just a few years earlier would have been shared by the Stewart and Cunningham families. The Redshanks along the Foyle could be considered as British subjects in an ecumenical Scottish sense, complete with appropriate loyalties and a version of the Protestant faith. In the Portlough precinct, the incoming Planter Scots came from Ayrshire and Lennox. Lennox included lands in the Scottish Gaeltacht and even parts of Ayrshire were still Gaelic speaking in the early 1600s. The Planter Scots from these areas were familiar with Gaelic language and customs and Redshanks were a familiar part of their world.

The muster rolls for the Portlough precinct in 1630 provide the first chance to locate the Redshanks. These Redshanks are not hard to find as their surnames give them away. By 1630 some of the original Planters had passed away, but members of the Stewart and Cunningham families still held the Portlough precinct and six of them appear in the Muster Rolls of that year along with the men from their lands that turned out for military service.

One of the families associated with Iníon Dubh is the Crawfords. The Crawfords were members of Iníon Dubh's bodyguard. Of the one hundred man company that comprised Iníon Dubh's personal bodyguard it is said as many as eighty of them were surnamed Crawford. To this day there are many

43

Crawfords in the Laggan and the lore of their origins is remembered in the district. It is possible that they were the Crawfords of Cumnock area of Ayrshire, as that particular Crawford family was part of the elaborate Caimbeul kinship network. The Caimbeuls of Loudon obtained the Crawford castle and lands of Terringzean, just outside of Cumnock, in Ayrshire, through marriage. Shortly after this event, in the late 1560s, the Crawfords emerge as the bodyguards of Iníon Dubh. Indeed, there are eight Crawford men that are listed in the 1630 Portlough muster roll.

The Crawfords served Clann Uí Dhónaill well and their military accomplishments are still remembered. In 1597 Eóin Crawford held the castle at Ballyshannon that protected the southern passage into Ó Dónaill lands. In July of that year, Conyers Clifford, the governor of Connaught, led an English army on a major offensive against the castle. Conyers amassed a sizeable force for the task comprised of 4,000 English troops, four cannon, and additional Irish allies. Eóin Crawford had only 80 men in his command. In the opening stages of the assault the English used their cannon to breach the castle walls. Eóin Crawford managed to fight off each assault attempting to force through the breach, inflicting heavy casualties on his enemy. After three days of battle the English withdrew after hearing rumours that Aodh Rua Ó Dónaill was approaching with a relief column. At the end of the engagement over 600 English soldiers were dead and three of their cannon and much of their supplies were captured.

Along with the Crawfords there are many surnames associated with the Caimbeul family on the 1630 muster roll. There are twenty-three Caimbeuls as well as a host of other surnames connected to the Caimbeuls as septs or allied families, such as Allan, MacArthur, MacClean, and MacCain. In addition to the mid Argyll Redshanks with Caimbeul connections there are also a large number of Redshanks from the Lennox District of Scotland and many of these also had connections to the family. In the mid 1500s Clann Chaimbeul expanded their sphere of influence into the Lennox lands around Loch Lomond. The Mac Griogair, Mac Pharláin, and Buchanan clans were drawn into Caimbeul alliances and these surnames are numerous in the muster rolls.[13] The Mac Griogairs in particular were noted for providing Redshanks for the Caimbeul military.

Given the number of Lennox Redshank families represented in the 1630 muster rolls it is likely that the Duke of Lennox and his kinsmen in the Portlough precinct brought additional Redshanks from the Lennox district of Scotland. The Redshanks from Lennox shared many qualities with the Argyll Redshanks. The Lennox district was part of the Highlands, but it was on the cusp of the Scottish Gaeltacht. The clans there were often bilingual, speaking both Gaelic and Lallans. The Lennox Gaels were exposed to the Reformed faith very early also, which certainly would have given them another common bond with the Caimbeul Redshanks. Like the Argyll Redshanks, the men from Lennox were an easy fit alongside the Ayrshire families arriving into the Portlough Precinct.

---

[13] Jane Dawson, *The Campbells are coming!: a 16th-Century experience. (A Campbell push into the Lennox and Menteith)*, The University of Edinburgh, unpublished lecture, http://www.ed.ac.uk/schools-departments /divinity/research/resources/breadalbane/historical-background/clan-campbell/references-publications

There is evidence that after the Plantation began in 1609 very little change happened in the Portlough precinct. There were new landlords to be sure as the Stewarts and the Cunninghams replaced the Ó Dónaills. The new settlers were not that far removed from the Redshanks already living there as can be observed by records from the early years of the Plantation. In an effort to civilize the natives the British government attempted to outlaw Gaelic dress in the area. However, the policy met with opposition from the Scottish settlers themselves. The items of clothing banned included tartan materials and plaids (a blanket worn in cooler weather and was also used in the filleadh mór or full kilt). This type of attire was considered Gaelic and therefore 'Irish' to English perceptions. The problem was this was also the clothing worn by the Ulster Scots, be they already established Redshanks or settlers new to the area.

In April of 1628 in the *Calendar of State Papers for Ireland* there is a letter from King James I concerning the state of the Stewart lands in the Portlough precinct. King James complains that, '(the Stewart lands) have not been duly planted.'[14] An observation followed by a threat of an inquiry into a breach of the condition of the grant. The lands had been planted in truth, but in a particularly Scottish style, which included the pre Plantation Redshanks along with the ethnically and culturally similar Ayrshire and Lennox Scots. Another example of the nature of the Scottish Plantation of the area is found in the *The Irish Commission of 1622* which includes a report upon the estate of Sir John Drummond, which

---

[14] Hans Claude Hamilton, ed., *Calendar of the State Papers Relating to Ireland 1625-1632*, (London: Longman, Green, Longman & Roberts, 1860) 323.

was located on the east side of the Foyle River across from Portlough precinct. The Drummond estate had 2 freeholders and 31 lease holders; the report comments, 'and to say truly all but four or five are redshanks who are for the most part but cottagers.'[15]

The Redshanks in the Laggan played a prominent part in the creation of the Ulster Scots community there. They were part of the Laggan army that defeated the Irish under Felim Ó Neill at the battle of Glenmaquin in June 1642. Glenmaquin was an epic battle in the Wars of the Three Kingdoms in which William and Robert Stewart soundly defeated Felim Ó Neill's invasion of east Donegal. The Stewarts were well trained soldiers and their troops disciplined and dedicated. The battle is often characterized as an Ulster Scots versus Irish engagement. However, the Irish forces on the field at Glenmaquin included a large number of Scottish Redshanks. The Irish army included the north Antrim Redshanks under Dónall Gorm Mac Dónaill and additional Hebridean Redshanks under Alasdair Mac Colla. It is ironic that they were defeated by a Laggan Ulster Scots army that also included a large number of Donegal Redshanks with Caimbeul connections. Irish lords meeting on the battlefield with their Redshank soldiers is a common theme in Ulster history, in this case, the scenario only changed by new lords, the Scottish Stewarts, taking the part of the Ó Dónaill lords of the past.

While the Laggan Redshanks became part of the larger Ulster Scot community there, it would be wrong to assume that

---

[15] Victor Treadwell, ed., The Irish Commission 1622, 572. Transcript of letter sent to the author by Dr. William Roulston.

the Laggan Redshanks lost their distinct Gaelic culture. As Dr. Peter Toner's research into the Gaeltachtaí (Gaelic speaking areas) in New Brunswick, Canada, demonstrates, many of these Donegal Presbyterians remained Gaelic speaking well into the twentieth century and this includes those that migrated to the New World.[16] It would have been an interesting world for the Redshank descendants in Donegal, many would have been bilingual in Gaelic and Lallans and they occupied a unique place among the native Irish and Plantation Scot communities. To this day it is very common to encounter Redshank surnames in the Donegal Gaeltacht and many of them have remained part of the traditional Gaelic community. The Redshanks in the Laggan are an interesting aspect of Irish history. They are certainly part of the Ulster Scots story, yet they are also part of an older Gaelic story.

---

[16] Peter M Toner, *Confusing Identities: The Gaeltachtaí In New Brunswick, 1901*. The Seventeenth Biennial Ulster-American Heritage Symposium, 25-28 June 2008. Centre for Migration Studies at the Ulster American Folk Park, Omagh, N Ireland.

7 Laggan Redshank Time Line

This time line includes the major military engagements of the Laggan Redshanks. There were countless small battles and skirmishes in which the Redshanks were employed, too many to mention. The nature of warfare in Ulster during this time was one of raid and counter raid. Large scale pitched battles were rare, but did happen from time to time. The Redshanks successfully defended the Ó Dónaill lands from many English raids as well as those done by rival clans from the mid 1500s until late 1601.

1569 August: Marriage of Fionnuala Nic Dhónaill (Iníon Dubh) to Aodh Mac Manus Ó Dónaill; over 1,000 Redshanks are part of Iníon Dubh's dowry. Iníon Dubh settles at Mongavlin in Portlough precinct, County Donegal.

1571 September: Iníon Dubh in Argyll to recruit more Caimbeul Redshanks.

1572 Birth of Aodh Rua Ó Dónaill.

1586 Iníon Dubh becomes the de facto leader of Clann Uí Dhónaill.

1587 Autumn: Capture of Aodh Rua Ó Dónaill by John Perrott.

1588 Iníon Dubh's Redshanks kill Aodh Mac Cabhlach Ó Dónaill after his unsuccessful attempt to seize the headship of Clann Uí Dhónaill.

1590 14 September: Battle of Derrylaghan County Donegal; Iníon Dubh and her Redshank army defeats Dónal Ó Dónaill. Dónal is killed along with many of his followers.

1591 24 December: Escape of Aodh Rua Ó Dónaill from Dublin Castle.

1592 May: Aodh Rua Ó Dónaill becomes taoiseach of Clann Uí Dhónaill.

1595 25-27 March: Battle of Clontibret, County Monahan; Irish victory, Aodh Rua Ó Dónaill and Aodh Ó Neill defeat Henry Bagenel, English suffer heavy losses.

1597 2-4 August: Battle of Ballyshannon, County Donegal; Irish victory, Eóin Crawford defeats Conyers Clifford with heavy English causalities and loss of cannon and baggage.

1598 14 August: Battle of the Yellow Ford, County Armagh; Irish victory, Aodh Rua Ó Dónaill, Aodh Ó Neill, and Aodh Mag Uidhir defeat Henry Bagnel, very heavy English losses and Bagnel killed.

1599 15 August: Battle of Curlew Pass, County Roscommon; Irish victory, Aodh Rua Ó Dónaill defeats Conyers Clifford, very heavy English casualties and Clifford killed.

1600 20 September: Battle of Moyry Pass, Counties Armagh and Louth; Stalemate, Aodh Rua Ó Neill, Aodh Ó Neill face Lord Mountjoy, heavy casualties on both sides.

1601 2 October – 3 January: 1602 Battle of Kinsale, County Cork; Decisive English victory, Aodh Rua Ó Dónaill,

Aodh Ó Neill, and Juan del Aguila, face Lord Mounjoy, heavy casualties on both sides.

1602 Aodh Rua Ó Dónaill travels to Spain to recruit aid to continue the war, but dies there in September. He is buried at the Franciscan monastery in Valladolid, Spain.

1607 The Flight of the Earls.

1609 Iníon Dubh retires to lands at Kilmacrennan.

1610 The Stewart and Cunninghams become the Undertakers for the Portlough precinct. Iníon Dubh's lands are taken over by Ludovic Stewart, the second Duke of Lennox.

1619 Pynar's survey of the Portlough precinct

1628 King James I's letter to Duke Lennox complaining that his lands have not been planted with settlers.

1630 The Portlough Redshanks and their descendants appear in the muster rolls of the Stewart and Cunningham families.

1642 16 June: Battle of Glenmaquin, County Donegal. The Portlough Redshanks are part of the Ulster Scots Laggan army under Robert and William Stewart that defeats the native Irish and Scottish Redshank army under Felim Ó Neill and Aladair Mac Colla Mhic Dhónaill.

8 1630 Portlough Precinct Muster Rolls

The 1630 Raphoe Muster rolls include those for the old Portlough precinct. Because every family living on these lands was expected to have their able bodied men report for the muster it provides a census of sorts for the district. The Portlough muster rolls reveal a large number of Redshank surnames and many of these have Clann Chaimbeul connections. The most relevant muster rolls concerning the Laggan Redshanks are those of the Stewarts and Cunningham families. These two families received their grants of the land in Portlough precinct in 1610-1611 and still held their lands when the muster rolls were taken in 1630. Some of the original Undertakers had passed away or sold their holdings to other family members, but these two families still held most of the precinct. The Undertakers on the muster rolls listed within the Portlough precinct were the Duke of Lennox, Lady Cunningham, William Stewart, Alexander Stewart, James Cunningham, and John Stewart.

Ludovic Stewart, the second Duke of Lennox, was an original Undertaker in Portlough precinct. Ludovic passed away in 1624. He was succeeded by his brother, Esmé Stewart the third Duke of Lennox, who also passed away in 1624. It was Esmé Stewart's son, James, who was the fourth Duke when the muster roll was taken for the Duke of Lennox's lands in Portlough precinct. Lady Cunningham was the widow of Sir James Cunningham who had an original grant of land. William Stewart was also an original Undertaker. Alexander Stewart, most sources say, purchased his land from Alexander MacAula, who was the Duke of Lennox's agent, though the latter also was known by the surname Stewart and the matter is not entirely clear. James Cunningham was an original Undertaker and John Stewart

was a son of the second Duke of Lennox. John Stewart is not listed on the original grants, but he held large portions of his father's lands, including Mongavlin Castle and the surrounding lands. He is listed as an Undertaker in Pynar's survey which was done in 1619. The Stewarts' lands were in the southern part of Portlough precinct and the Cunninghams' lands were in the northern part.

The Stewarts' land, and specifically the holding of the Duke of Lennox, are particularly revealing in providing an idea of the numbers of Redshanks still in this part of the Laggan. James I, or his agents, judged that the Duke's land had not been planted at all as late as spring 1628. For this reason, the Duke's muster roll gives a very good idea of the numbers of pre Plantation Redshanks in the area. The Duke had 162 men turn out for the muster and around 57 per cent of these men have Redshank surnames, which is the highest percentage of all six Portlough undertaker rolls.

The four Stewarts on the rolls have more men in their muster than the Cunninghams and more Redshanks. The Stewarts had 269 men turn out and around 52 percent are obvious Redshanks. The Cunninghams had 125 turn out with about 31 per cent of obvious Redshank origin. In the aggregate around 50 percent of the Portlough precinct muster were Redshanks. Again, that figure cannot be exact, because of the complete lack of consistency in anglicised forms of Gaelic origin surnames. The actual percentage of Redshanks could be much higher.

In estimating the percentages of Redshanks on the rolls the many Stewart surnames are not counted. One could argue that the Lennox Stewarts are a Highland Scottish family, but they would not have been in the ranks of the Redshanks that came in with Iníon Dubh. A few west Lowland Scottish surnames can be included, such as Crawford. The Portlough Precinct muster rolls with the spellings left as they appeared:

1. The Lord Duke of Lynox, undertaker of 4000 acres, his men and armes

Swords Only

Robert Leackye	William Laughlan
James Wood	John Lowrye
Andrew Wood	John Ralston
Mathew Lyndsey	William Cokeran
William Douglas	Hector Hinman
Robert Lyndsay	Robert Cocheran
Robert Buchanan	John Buchanan
John Galbreath	John mcConochy
Alexander Buchanan	Robert mcPeter
Alexander Lawder	George Haldin
James Denniston elder	Robert Horner
Andrew Royare	Donell Galey

Robert mcKyndely
Robert Glass
Archbell Campbell
ffyndley mcKindley
Andrew mctyre
Alexander Galbreath
John mcKaire
John Thromble
John Smyth
Dunkan mcffarlen
Patrick mcNeron
Wm. McLentock
George Colmories
Robert mcffarlan

John mcffarlan
Patt mcAndrew
Patt. mcArthur
Robert Denyston
Donnell mcBaxter
John Boyd
Humfrey Colquphone
William Gulilan
John Steward
John McIlman
John Scot
Robert Boyde
Thomas Lowrye

Swords and Snaphances
John Wood
John Martin
John mcLenochan
John Cambell elder
William Deneston
John Buchanan
John Cambell
John mcffarlan
Donnell mcffarlan
Robert Michell
Costyme Ranckein
John Allen
Gilbert mcLyntock
John Brice

James Allan
Dunkan Speney
Thomas Ramsey
John Cock
James Cock
Andrew Cock
William Scot
John mcCawly
John mcGourden
Andrew Lackye
James mcKennye
James Hustone
Robert Lackye

Snaphances Only

James Dromond   Archbald Gambell

Swords and Pikes

Morrice mcConnell   James Kilsoe
John Cocheran   Donnell mcNichol
John Snodgarse   Dunkan Cambell
John Cambell younger   Donnell mcBaxter elder
Owen mcNair   Robert Barlaine
David Lyndsay   James Richye
Alexander mcLentock   John Swayne
Robert Aickeene   John Valentyne
Robert Morison   Dunkan Graham

Pikes Only

Robert Calmeris   Andrew Calmeris

Sword and Halbert

Hugh Greire

Sword and Calleuer

John mcffarlan

No Arms

John Royer,   John mcIldonagh
Morrice Peacock   Dunkan mcffarlan
Walter Lowrye   John Crawfford
William mcNevin   John Sempell
Robert Campbell   James Symison
John mcKyndley   William mcarthur
David mcKan   Robert Reroch

Thomas Crafford
Camack mcCole
Henry Cruse
John Barlone
Thomas Swaine
Patrick Porlerm
Randall mcAlexander
John Douglas
James Logan
Alexander Hamond
Mathew Gillrew
William Hewes
Robert Leman
Donnell mcCahey
Adam Quahone
Neece mcGilrouse
John mcffarlan
Walter Deneston
Anthony Steward
William Noble
John Parmenter
Andrew Galbreath
Willliam Wood

John Wood
John Steward
James Deneston
James Muthey
John Pecock
Walter Roger
Robert Craufourd
John Brittein
Archbald Ballintyne
John Young
Thomas mcKeeg
Gawen mcConnell
John Logan
John Watson
Lamock mcColl
Walter Henry
John Buchanan
Robert Cambell
David Gibb
Dunkan Crafford
John Pearce
George Allyson
John mcGillione

2. The Lady Conningham Widdow of Sir James Conningham, undertaker of 2,000 acres, her men and armes.

Swords and Pikes
William Conningham
James Calquahan
Andrew mcCorkill

John mcCorkill
Tobias Hood
James Davye

Peter Starret
John mcquchowne

James Knox
Adam Garvance

Swords and Snaphances
James mcAdowe
ffyndlay Ewing
Dunkan mcffarlan
Ninian ffoulton
James Scot

William Rankin
Daniell Ramsay
Martin Galbreath
Patrick Porter

Swords and Calleuers
William mcIltherne
David Walker

John Barbor

Sword and Halbert
James Makee

Swords Only
Andrew George
James mcIlman
Michaell Rot[h?]es
Patrick Miller
Robert Muntgomery
Alexander Conningham
Richard Leaky

Robert Staret
John mcIlhome
Sallomon Giffin
David Reed
Donnell mcDonnell
Alexander Carlell
William Gafeth

No Arms
Gilbert Highgate
Patrick Porter
Robert Hasta
William Gambell
John Hunter

John Crawfford
Robert Johnston
Henry Smyth
William Boyes
David Ramsay

William Steward

Robert Crafford

James Conningham

Andrew Conningham

John Crafford

John Hunter

John Wilson

James Bredyne

Mungo Davy

William Richey

John mcIlhome

Henry Hunter

John mcHutchon

James Rankin

William Killy

Robert Pots

William Gambell

John Lyone

James Knox

3. William Steward Esqr. Lard of Dunduff, undertaker of 1,000 acres, his men and armes.

Swords Only

Archbald Thomson

Andrew Thompson

Robert Alexander

John mcKey

David Kenedye

Patrick Baruzathyn

Anthony Steward

John Steward

Archbald Steward

John Browne

Andrew Browne

Edward Roger

John Moore,

John mcCullagh

John Moire

Patrick Conningham

John Allyson

John Smeally

Swords and Pikes

John Davidson

Archbald mcEmmory

Roary mcCleane

Patrick Thomson

Donnell Or

Mungo David

John Cambell

John mcLynienie

Archbald Hourd

William Houston

James mcKee

Anthony Kenedy

George Steward

John mcClen

John Cambell

Hugh Gamill

Swords and Muskets

Robert Thomson

John ffife

Swords and Snaphances

James Squire

John Conningham

Steaphen Marshell

John Smyth

Michaell Smith

Michaell mcCleary

Donnell Cambell

Archbald Bredene

No Arms

John Kelly

Humphrey Cooke

William Wan

ffynley mcKirdly

Alexander mcClaney

John Conningham

John mcffay

Donnell mcNevin alias McNit

John mcKee younger

John mcWalker

James mcKergour

David Kenedy

Alexander mcWilliam

Patrick Steward

Donnell mcCarslaire

James Kenellye

John Campbell

4. Mr. Alexander Steward, undertaker of 1,000 acres, his men and armes.

Swords and Pikes

John mcIlwane

Callum mcMuyre

James Cambell

Robert mcKenily

William To[y]es

William Conningham

William Home   Alexander Cambell

Neall mcCurid

Swords and Snaphances

Alexander Cambell   Robert Boyd

John mcKenely   Robert Henedy

Storiment Carr

Sword and Musket

John Niweme younger

Sword and Target

Walter mcffarlen

Swords Only

John Kennan   Ninian Steward

No Arms

Andrew Cambell   James ffyfe

Gilbert mcKenny   Arch Alexander

John Gillaspy   John Roger

Robert Steward   John Boyill

John Steward   William Boyill

Archbald Steward   John Cambell

William Cambell   Gilbert mcCan

5. James conningham Esqr. undertaker of 1,000 acres, his men and armes.

Swords Only

Andrew Crafford   John Gills

Hugh Lokehart

Arch ffynlagh

Swords and Pikes

John Alexander

Snaphances Only

Andrew Arnott

John Alexander

Swords and Snaphances

John Smyth

William Gall

Andrew Smyth

James Gillmore

Robert Roger

Swords and Halberts

Robert mcKeene

No Arms

James ffulloone

George Steavenson

Joseph Browne

William Galbreath

Hugh Leag

Andrew Browne

John Harper

Thomas Stole

Patrick Robison

John Enery

ffynlay mcCredy

John Browne

George White

Adnarle Hoomes

Robert Graham

Thomas Roger

Thomas Lars

John Adam

Robert Davison

Michaeli Beare

Mathew Giesse

Andrew Leag

John Hururence

John Hamilton

James ffulloone

Robert Patterson

John Cunningham

George Naught

Hugh Leag

James Browne

John mcEuan

George Speare

Dunkan mcWrick

Mathew mcCadame

Thomas Richmoule

John Dyne

John mcJohn Keine

Andrew Dyne

Mungo Willy

Arch Boyle

Andrew Cambell

John Calwell

Hugh Mure

Robert mcCamy

Andrew Callhow

Robert mcCamy younger

6. Mr. John Steward, undertaker of 1,000 acres, his men and armes.

Swords Only

Arch Steward

Illime mcKaine

Andrew Cambell

James ffife

William Cambell

John Steward

Pike Only

John Barkly

Sword and Snaphance

William Conningham

Sword and Pike

John Bullesine

Pike Only

Robert Steward

John Boyle

John Roger

Arch Alexander

Notes on arms listed:

Calleuer: a firearm, better known as a Caliver. It is usually a matchlock weapon that was lighter and shorter than a musket. It had a standardized bore which gave the soldier access to a standard round. The caliver was easier to reload than a musket and could fire two rounds in the time it took a musket to fire one. It had less penetration power and range than the musket. The weight of the caliver was around ten pounds.

Halberd: a two handed pole weapon. At the top was an axe topped by a spike. The length of halberds varied between six to eight feet.

Musket: the standard battlefield firearm. It was a heavy matchlock weapon that weighed around eighteen pounds and needed a rest to help the soldier steady and hold the weapon when used.

No Arms: weapons were expensive in the seventeenth century as they are now. Many men reported for duty who did not possess a weapon. They would be outfitted with a wide assortment of makeshift weapons, usually some sort of pike or half pike, while others would use farm implements or even clubs.

Pike: a very long thrusting spear used by infantry. The length varied and could be as short as ten feet or as long as eighteen feet.

Snaphance: an early form of flintlock firearm. It was expensive and cutting edge battlefield technology in the early 1600s. The snaphance functioned better in damp weather than other firearms used at this time. It was a lighter weapon than a musket and the soldier did not need a rest to fire it. It could be reloaded faster than a musket.

Swords: most were broad swords and many of the men who carried them would have the distinctive wooden shield commonly called a targe in Ireland and Scotland. The distinctive Irish hilt sword, also called a basket hilt sword, was also in use during this time.

Epilogue

While outside the scope of this short history, the 1642 muster rolls for Raphoe, which include the Portlough precinct, reflect an influx of post 1630 Scottish Lowland settlers. Many of these settlers were refugees from other parts of Ulster that fled to the Laggan for protection after the Uprising broke out in 1641. The Redshanks do still appear in the 1642 rolls and in considerable numbers, but there were new waves of Ulster Scots coming into the Laggan. The market towns, such as St Johnston, were dominated by the new arrivals. Lallans became the main language in time and the memory of the remarkable Redshanks and their legacy faded into the lore of the district.

When the Ulster Migration to the America Colonies began in 1718 many of the early immigrants that went to the Colonies were from the Laggan. The co-leader of the first fleet was James McKeen, who was a descendant of the Redshanks that settled in the Portlough precinct. His in-law and co-leader was Rev James MacGregor, another Ulsterman with Redshank roots. There was a considerable Redshank presence in what we now call the Scots-Irish in America. The stereotypical view of the Scots-Irish is that they 'all' descend from Lowland planters that arrived in Ulster after 1609. The reality is that many

Scots-Irish have Highland Scottish ancestry as evidenced by even a casual examination of common Scots-Irish surnames.

Starting in the early 1830s another wave of Ulster immigrants, including many Laggan folk, began a migration to Canada that was even larger than the eighteenth Century migration to the Colonies. Many of these families settled in northern New Brunswick. As mentioned, Dr. Peter Toner's research into the Protestant Gaelic speaking towns and villages in New Brunswick from 1851 into the early twentieth Century reveals fascinating insights into the culture of these west Ulster families in Canada. Many of these Protestant Irish settlers into New Brunswick in the mid 1800s came from east Donegal and were still Irish speaking. Linguistically the Irish spoken in Donegal, especially the Irish that was spoken in east Donegal, was much influenced by Hebridean and Argyll Gaelic, a legacy of the Redshanks.

The story of the Laggan Redshanks is an important aspect of the history of both Ireland and Scotland. Their history is an integral part of the shared traditions and links between Ulster and Scotland. Their descendants continue to be a vital part of Ulster society and are found everywhere Ulster folk have settled around the world. It is my hope that this short history will not only help the memory of these Redshanks to endure, but will also stimulate more research about them and their society.

Appendix I

This appendix is an alphabetized Portlough precinct muster roll with notes on many of the surnames. Mc is written as Mac. Many of the surnames have multiple origins, but this list is done with the knowledge that these men were almost exclusively Scottish. The list will give the reader an idea of the origins of the Ulster Scots in the Laggan prior to 1630. Many of the surnames are not 'clan' surnames, but rather names from traditional Scottish patronymics and other naming customs. However, some clan surnames do appear on the list, such as those associated with Clann Chaimbeul and Clann Mhic Giolla Eáin.

Most of the surnames have a Gaelic etymology, while a few have Norman, Norse, or other origins. Having a Norman surname does not necessarily mean a family is of Norman origin. Indigenous Scots borrowed names from the cultures to which they were exposed. DNA testing can tell if a family is of Celtic ancestry or Norman ancestry. This list will be of use for readers who have participated in the Y chromosome DNA testing. If one has a Y chromosome DNA match to a family from the Laggan district and has a surname from the list, this will provide a line of research.

These surnames were recorded at a time when Gaelic surnames were being anglicised in official records. Some were anglicised to an English form that was a phonetic rendering of how the name sounded in Gaelic. Other surnames were given an English or Lallans form that was only vaguely similar in sound to the original Gaelic name. Some names were simply translated, such as Mac Gabhann, which became 'Smith.' Several names are difficult to decipher what the original Gaelic form was and only an educated guess is provided. Common modern anglicised forms are in parenthesis following the surnames and if relevant a link to a related name.

Adam (Adam, Adams, MacAdam) This is a common Scottish name and is from Mac Adaim.

Aickeene (Aitken) General to Scotland; it is an anglicised form of Mac Aidicín a diminutive form of Adam.

Allan, Allen (MacAllen) Usually from Argyll and connected to Clann Chaimbeul, in Gaelic Mac Ailein. The Gaelic root word is Ail meaning 'rock.' The English surname Allan has a different etymology and is from a Breton name taken from a German tribal name Alemannus meaning 'all men.'

Allyson (Allison) A Scottish surname name with several theories concerning its origin and it possibly has more than one origin. In the Scottish Highlands Allison is an anglicised form of Alasdair. In other parts of Scotland it may be a loan word taken from the Hebrew name Elijah turned into a patronymic, i.e. Eli's son. Some researchers have even suggested it is a patronymic of the Norse name Olaf. The surname is associated with Clann Dhónaill and Clann Mhic Pharláin.

Arnott This is a toponymic surname from the lands of Arnot in Kinross-shire, Scotland, from the Gaelic word Ornacht meaning 'barley.'

Ballentine A Scottish toponymic origin surname that first appeared in Lanarkshire; it is from the Gaelic Baile an Deadhain meaning 'village of the dean.'

Ballintyne (see Ballentine)

Barbor (Barbour) A Scottish name which is from the French word Barbier an occupational name, i.e. a barber.

Barkly Thought to be an English toponymic surname in origin, but established in Scotland by the late 1200s; from Aberdeenshire and Fife.

Barlaine This is probably a rendering of Parlan as in Mac Pharláin.

Baruzathyn (Brabazon) A Norman origin surname which is from 'le Brabazoun,' i.e. a native of Brabant in Flanders.

Beare (Barr) This is a toponymic Scottish surname which comes from the Gaelic word Barr, meaning 'top' or 'height.' In Scotland it is often from Barr in Ayrshire or Barr in Renfrewshire.

Boyd Usually from Argyll and Bute and derived from Eilean Bhoid, 'isle of Bute.' Several Boyd families in the Ulster Heritage DNA Project confirmed Bute origins in their test results.

Boyes In Donegal often an anglicised form Ó Baothghalaigh, 'son of Baothghalach' (foolhardy).

Boyill (Boyle) There are several origins of this surname; in Donegal it is from Ó Baoighill, meaning descendant of Baoigheall, 'vain pledge.' It is also an Ayrshire surname thought to have a Norman in etymology from the toponymic name Beauville.

Bredyne (Breden) Probably from Mac Bradáin or Ó Bradáin, from the root word Bradan meaning salmon.

Brice A Scottish surname which is from the Latin forename Bricius, the name of fifth-century saint from Gaul popular in Scotland.

Brittein A Lowland surname that generally shows distant ancestry from Brittany. Bretons comprised a large element of the Norman military and ruling elites that came to England in and after AD 1066. Many 'Normans' that were settled in Scotland were actually Bretons.

Browne This surname has multiple origins in Scotland. It can be from the Norse, Old English, and Norman French, word Brun meaning 'brown,' or it can be from the Gaelic Donn also meaning 'brown.' Additionally, many Highlanders connected with the position of a Breitheamh (a traditional Gaelic judge) anglicised their surname as Browne.

Buchanan This is a Lennox toponymic surname from the eastern shores of Loch Lomond on the cusp of the Highlands. The Buchanans were associated with Lord Lennox and were also Clan Chaimbeul allies from which they recruited their Redshanks. The etymology is thought to be from the Gaelic words Buth (house) and Canan (canon, as in a church official).

Bullesine (see Ballentine)

Callhow Another difficult name to decipher, but probably a butchered form of the Scottish name Colquhoun.

Calmeris This surname is from the Gallowayshire in the southwest Lowlands. It was originally Mac Ó Calmery. I was not able to ascertain its meaning.

Calwell An anglicised from of the Gaelic surname Mac Cathmaoil, 'son of the Cathmhaol,' or Battle chief.

Campbell From Argyll; one of the great clans of Scotland, the Gaelic spelling is Caimbeul meaning 'wry mouthed.'

Carlell (Carlisle) This name is habitational Scottish name and a form of Carlisle.

Carr (Kerr) This anglicised form has several origins, but in this case it is probably from the name Ciar, which is Gaelic for 'brunette haired man.' The name is often originally from Arran, Ayrshire, or Bute.

Cock This is a Lowland surname which is probably Cumbric in origin; 'Coch' means Red, as in hair colour.

Cokeran (Cocheran) Usually a toponymic surname from Renfrewshire of unknown origin, but it is also an anglicised form used by an Argyll family surnamed Mac Eachthigheirn when they migrated to the Lowlands.

Colmories An anglicised form hard to decipher; it is possibly a crudely anglicised form of Cill Mhoire meaning the 'cell of Mary,' as in a place of worship dedicated to the Virgin Mary. There are several Cill Mhoire place names in Argyll.

Colquphone (Calhoun) From Lennox; according to Clan Calhoun lore the name is taken from the Gaelic Coille Chumhann, meaning 'narrow wood.' The Calhouns were a powerful clan on the borders of the Scottish Gaeltacht.

Conningham (Cunningham) An intriguing habitational surname originally from Ayrshire. There are several theories of the origin; one is the surname is from the Gaelic Cuinneag meaning 'milk pail,' and Ham, which is the northern English word for settlement or village.

Cooke An occupational surname of Scottish origin, taken from the Latin word Cocus meaning 'cook.'

Crawfford (Crawford) A habitational surname from Ayrshire and Lanarkshire; a large number of Crawfords settled in the Portlough precinct in 1569. They were Iníon Dubh's personal bodyguard company and served under Aodh Rua Ó Dónaill. The etymology is thought to be from the Lallans word Craw (a crow) and Ford (as in the crossing of a river).

Cruse (Cruise) A surname with two possible origins; one is from the Cymreag word Cryw meaning 'stepping stones' or from medieval English name Crouse meaning 'a bold man.'

Davidson (David, Davison) From the Gaelic name Mac Dáibhidh.

Davye, Davy Nickname forms of Mac Dáibhidh.

Denniston (Dennison) From the Western Lowlands and Argyll. The origin of this surname often is linked to the name Dennis, but given its geographical origin Mac Donnchaidh is the likely etymology.

Douglas A western Lowlands name thought to have originated in Lanarkshire. The name is from the Gaelic Dubh (black) Glais (water or stream). The Douglas clan was powerful and important in Scottish history.

Dromond (Drummond) From Lennox; Druimeanich in Gaelic. The lore of the clan of this name is a romantic one with links to a Hungarian prince, but DNA testing has confirmed most Drummonds are indigenous Insular Celts native to Scotland.

Dyne (Dean) In Ulster this is normally an anglicised form of Mac Deagáin, 'son of the dean.' It other parts of Ireland it is often an anglicised form of Ó Dúinín from a diminutive of Donn meaning 'brown.'

Enery An anglicised form of the Argyll surname Mac Eanruig 'son of Henry' and Mac Énrí, which also means 'son of Henry.'

Ewing This is another anglicised form of Mac Eogháin.

ffife (Fife) A Scottish habitational surname from Fife, Scotland.

ffoulton (Fulton)   A southeast Lowland surname, originally found in Roxburghshire from Old English Fugol (bird) and Tun (enclosure).

ffulloone (Folane)   While this is a difficult anglicised form to decipher it phonetically resembles the surname Mac Fualáin meaning 'son of the Faolan;' a diminutive of Faol or 'wolf.'

ffynlagh (Finlay)   Anglicised form of the Gaelic name Fionnlaoch from the two words Fionn (white or fair) and Laoch (hero). It is general to Scotland.

Gafeth   Hard to decipher; possibly a form of the Redshank surname Mac Dhaibhidh or even from the Welsh Dafydd (David).

Galbreath (Galbraith)   From Lennox; the modern Gaelic form is Mac an Breathnaigh, 'son of the Briton' that is a Scot that descended from the Cumbric Celtic people of Scotland. Historian Tim Clarkson has theorized that this name may literally be Gall Breathnach or 'foreign Briton' and signify a group of Britons from the medieval kingdom of Strathclyde that were essentially Vikings, much like the Gall Ghaeil (Gaelic Vikings) circa AD 1050 to 1200.

Galey (MacGawley)   Anglicised form of Mag Amhalaí.

Gall   In Ulster and Scotland this can be an anglicised form of Mac an Ghaill 'son of the foreigner.'

Gambell (Campbell)   Argyll; there is a distinct 'Gambell' surname in Ulster which comes from an Norse forename of Gamal however in this case Gambell is likely a variant anglicised form of Caimbeul which was numerous in west Ulster at this time.

Gamill   A Lowland Scottish; from the Norse name Gamal meaning 'the old one.'

Garvance   A difficult name to decipher; it probably incorporates the Gaelic word Garbh (rough) as an element.

George The Gaelic form is Seóirse.

Gibb A diminutive of Gilbert and general to Scotland.

Giesse Very likely a mangled anglicised form of a Gaelic surname. Giesse is also a Silesian German surname and while not likely it is possibly of that origin.

Giffin (MacGiffin) From the Gaelic surname Mag Dhuibhfinn, 'son of black haired Fionn.' Mag is a form of Mac.

Gillaspy (Archibald, Gillespie) From the Gaelic name Giolla Easpuig, 'servant of the bishop.'

Gillmore From the Gaelic surname Mac Giolla Mhuire. Found throughout the Hebrides and Highlands; it means 'servant of the Virgin Mary.'

Gillrew Difficult to decipher, but probably from the Gaelic surname Mac Giolla Rua, 'servant of the red haired man.'

Gills Anglicised from the Gaelic surname Mac Giolla Íosa meaning 'servant of Jesus.'

Glass From the Gaelic name Glas, meaning 'grey.' The habit of using colour epithets was common in the Highlands and often evolved into a surname.

Graham Argyll, Lennox, and the Lowlands; the origin is Old English from Gran (gravel) and Ham (home); it became a habitational surname brought to Scotland by the Normans.

Greire (Greer, Greir) Lennox; a form of Mac Griogair.

Gulilan (Gillilan) Argyll; from Mac Giolla Fhaoláin (son of the servant of Saint Faolan).

Haldin Scottish, but its origins obscure; possibly a Lowland name coming from the forename Halfdan 'half Dane.' It is also found as MacAlden.

Hamilton The etymology of Hamilton is from Old English, Hamel (bare) Dun (hill), but many Hamiltons are of Norman origin. Walter FitzGilbert de Hameldone, was a Norman baron who gave his support to Robert the Bruce in the 13th Century. Many of the Hamiltons that settled in the Laggan were related to the Scottish Abercorn family.

Hamond Generally a Lowland surname; from the Norse Hámundr meaning 'high protection' and introduced to Scotland by the Normans.

Harper A Lennox surname associated with clan Buchanan. The etymology is from the old French Harpeor meaning a 'harp player.'

Hasta Another difficult surname to decipher, possibly from Mac hOisete meaning 'son of Hodge' a pet form of the name Roger. Hasta is normally rendered today as Hosty.

Henedy (see Kenedye)

Henry Multiple origins in both Ireland and Scotland. DNA testing shows that many Henry families descend from a mid-Argyll Mac Eanruig family, but others are from the native Irish Mac Enrí and still others are of Lowland origin.

Hewes (Hughs) General to the Highlands and Lowlands; a spelling of Hughes from twin Celtic origins; from the Gaelic Aodh and the Cumbric Huw, both from an old Celtic word meaning 'fire.'

Highgate While often considered an English origin surname in fact many Highgate families are from Ayrshire.

Hinman An odd Scottish surname found in Renfrewshire and other scattered places including Argyll. Possibly from the old English word Hine meaning 'servant.'

Home (also Hoomes, Holmes) A Scottish surname with two separate origins. One origin is from the Gaelic surname Mac Thóm, 'son of Thom' and the second is a habitational name from the Norse word Hulm meaning a 'small piece of land surrounded by a stream or river.'

Hood A surname with two origins in Ulster; from the Gaelic surname Ó hUid, a family associated with Clann Aodha Buí and from the English origin surname Hood meaning 'a maker of hoods.'

Horner Normally an English surname, but also found in the Scottish Lowlands. An occupational surname for a man who made or sold objects of horn.

Hourd An obscure surname of English origin from an Anglo Saxon word for 'grey haired.'

Hunter Primarily an Ayrshire origin name, but also found in Argyll; from the Gaelic Mac an tSealgair, 'son of the hunter.'

Hururence It is very difficult to know what the clerk meant by this attempt at writing a surname, possibly the name Ó Toráin, a Derry surname anglicised normally as Torrence, but that is a guess at best.

Hustone (Houston) In Gaelic Mac Úistin; from Hutchin a diminutive of Hugh.

Johnston (Johnson) Usually an Argyll origin surname; from Mac Eáin. Eáin is a Scots Gaelic dialect form of Eóin from the Latin name Iohannes. Johnston is also an anglicised form of Mac Seáin also from the Latin Iohannes, but via the Norman French form of Iohannes which is Jean.

Keine (Cain, Kane, Kean, Keen) From the surnames Ó Catháin and Mac Catháin from the given name Cathan meaning 'battler,' i.e. warrior.

Kelly An anglicised form of Mac Ceallaigh meaning 'son of Ceallach' (contention); common in the southwest Lowlands especially Gallowayshire.

Kenedye (Kennedy) An Ayrshire Gaelic surname from Cinnéidigh, which means 'grim headed' which refers to a dour or serious man or perhaps as Patrick Woulfe suggested a 'helmeted man.'

Kenellye (Kinneally) From of the Gaelic surname Mac Cinnfhaolaidh meaning 'descendant of Ceannfhaoladh' or 'wolf's head.' Generally regarded as a native Irish surname, but it could certainly be from the Scottish Gaeltacht.

Kennan From Mac Fhionnáin, 'son of Fionnán' (a diminutive of Fionn).

Killy (see Kelly)

Kilsoe (Kelso) The etymology is from the Cumbric name Calchfyndd meaning 'lime mountain;' a location associated with Kelso in Roxburghshire, Scotland. However, early examples of this surname are from Arran and Ayrshire.

Knox A well-known Scottish habitational name from De Cnoc or 'of the hill.'

Lars A Scottish form of Laurens an early saint's name.

Laughlan (MacLachlan) Argyll; from Mac Lachlainn. The root is Lachlann which was an old Gaelic name for Norway.

Lawder Possibly a family from Berwickshire in eastern Scotland, but this surname is also the anglicised form of the pet Gaelic name Láidir (strong) and may have origins in either Lennox or Argyll.

Leackye, (Lackye, Leaky, Leckie,) From the Gaelic word for slate or a slab of stone; in origin a habitational surname from the barony of Leckie in the parish of Gargunnock in Stirlingshire, but later found in Lennox. A branch of Clann Mhic Gríogair that settled in counties Donegal and Derry used the name.

Leag From the Scottish name Mac Coise 'son of the courier or footman' from the Gaelic word Cos meaning 'leg.'

Leman (Leaman, Lemon) Lennox and Argyll; an anglicised form of Mac Laghmainn meaning 'son of Laghmann;' a Norse personal name meaning a 'lawman, i.e. lawyer.'

Logan A habitational surname from the Gaelic Lagan meaning 'lowland' as in a dell or low area next to a river or body of water. Often an Ayrshire surname.

Lokehart (Lockart) A Scottish surname from Ayrshire and Lanarkshire of uncertain origin. The most colourful theory is that the surname is associated with Robert I. The King requested that upon his death that his heart be taken on a Crusade to aid in the fight against the enemies of Christ. It was a Sir Simon who did the task and he took the name 'Lock Heart' to honour the deed. Other theories abound; it is possibly from the Germanic name comprised of Loc (a lock) and Hard (as in hardy or brave) an occupational name for a herder who watched penned livestock. An alternative theory is a topographical surname from Loch Ard (Gaelic for high lake).

Lowrye (Lowry) Lennox; from Labhradha (spokesman) originally associated with Clann Mhic Labhrainn, but by the 1500s also linked to Clann Mhic Griogair.

Lyndsey (Lindsay) A surname with two origins; one is a Norman habitational name from De Limesay north of Rouen in France. The second origin more relevant in the Laggan is Lindsay was a name taken by some Mac Giolla Fhionntóg (MacClintock) families when they anglicised their surname.

Lyone From the Latin Leo meaning a 'lion;' a Lowland surname often from Ayrshire and Lanarkshire.

MacAdowe (MacDoo) An anglicised form of the Gaelic surname Mac Chonduibh, 'son of Cú dubh' (the black hound). MacAdoo is a common modern form.

MacAlexander (Alexander) General to all of Scotland, but particularly popular in Argyll, Ayrshire, and Hebrides; it is the anglicised form of Mac Alasdair, also written Mac Alsandair. The etymology goes back to the Greek name Alexander and means 'defender of men.'

MacAndrew (Andrew) A common Argyll surname, but found throughout the Scotland. It is an anglicised form of Mac Aindriú. From the Greek name Andrew meaning 'manly.'

MacArthur A common patronymic surname and is usually from mid Argyll; from the Gaelic surname Mac Artair meaning 'son of the bear' or 'bear-like.' The etymology is somewhat obscure, but is probably from a Celtic word for 'bear;' Arth in Cymreag and Art in Gaelic.

MacBaxter (Baxter) From Argyll; it is from the surname Mac an Bhacstair meaning 'son of the baker.' Lore links this family to Clann Mhic Mhaoláin.

MacCadame An anglicised form of Mac Adaim.

MacCahey (MacCaughey) This is an Argyll surname from the Gaelic Mac Eachaidh, a form of Mac Eachaidh, an ancient Gaelic name meaning 'horse man.'

MacCamy Anglicised form of the Gaelic surname Mac Shiamaidh, 'son of Siamaidh' a diminutive of Seamus.

MacCan (MacCann) This surname is problematic because several similar sounding Gaelic surnames are anglicised as MacCann. Usually it is an anglicised form of Mac Canna, also written Mac Anna. It means 'son of Annadh' an ancient Gaelic forename meaning 'wolf cub.' The Mac Canna family originated and ruled a district on the southern shores of Loch Neagh. DNA testing has shown also that MacCann is sometimes a nonstandard anglicised form of Mac Eáin.

MacCarslaire An anglicised form of Mac Artair.

MacCawly (MacCauley) From Argyll and Lennox; from the Gaelic Mac Amhlaoibh, 'son of Amhlaoibh' a Gaelicised form of the Norse name Olaf.

MacClaney This is another anglicised form of Mac Giolla Eáin, but with a Gaelic suffix of 'igh' on the end, i.e. Mac Giolla Eáinigh.

MacCleane (MacClain, MacClane, MacLain) This name in Gaelic is Mac Giolla Eáin meaning 'son of the servant of Iohannes.' It is native to the island of Mull in the Hebrides. Clann Mhic Ghiolla Eáin sent large numbers of Redshanks to Ireland in the 1500s and many settled there.

MacCleary A common Gaelic name which is an anglicised form of Mac an Chléirich meaning 'son of the clerk.' It is a surname native to both Argyll and the Isles, and to the western Lowlands, especially Ayrshire and Gallowayshire.

MacClen This is probably a form of Mac Fhloinn or 'son of Flann (ruddy haired).

MacCole (MacColl) This is the anglicised form of at least two Gaelic surnames; an Argyll name Mac Dhubhghaill meaning 'son of the dark haired foreigner' and Mac Giolla Chomhghaill, 'servant of Comgall' which is native to Donegal.

MacConnell (MacDonald, MacDonnell) This is the Gaelic surname Mac Dónaill with a seimhú after the initial D making it Mac Dhónaill. Writers in the seventeenth century often represented this sound change with the letter C.

MacConochy (MacConaghy) This is an anglicised from of Mac Dhonnadhaidh. It is common to all of Scotland, but in Ulster usually from Argyll. From Donnchadh meaning 'brown warrior.'

MacCorkill From the Gaelic, Mac Thorcaill, a shortened form of Mac Thorcadail (son of Thorketill); a Norse origin name meaning 'Thor's kettle.'

MacCredy (MacCready) A Gaelic surname that can be either Irish or Scottish and is from Mac Riada. Riada is a very old Gaelic name and is a contraction of Righ Fada or 'Long,' as in duration and 'King.' There was a family of Airchinnigh of this surname native to Donegal. Some Airchinnigh converted to the Protestant faith after the Church lands were confiscated during the early stages of the Plantation.

MacCullagh (MacCullough) Two similar sounding Scottish Gaelic names are anglicised as MacCullagh; one is from Mac Cullaich, meaning 'son of the boar' which is from Gallowayshire. The other is the Argyll surname Mac Lulaich, 'son of Lulach,' which comes from and old Gaelic name Lu Laogh meaning 'little calf.'

MacCurid This is probably an anglicised form of Mac Gothraidh. The modern anglicised form is MacCurry; the habit of putting the letter 'd' on the end of anglicised forms is not uncommon as irritating as it is. Another example of this is Mac Dónaill which becomes MacDonald when anglicised or MacKeand which is a Gallowayshire form of Mac Eáin. Another possible etymology of this name is Mac Mhuircheartaigh; anglicised commonly as MacCurdy today.

MacDonnell Anglicised form of Mac Dónaill. An old Gaelic surname that means 'world rule' and is probably from the Cumbric forename Dyfnwal.

MacEmmory (MacEmery, Amory) A Scottish surname believed to originate from the old German given name Amalric.

MacEuan A common Argyll surname and also found throughout much of Scotland. It is the anglicised form of

Mac Eogháin meaning 'son of Eoghan' an old Gaelic forename meaning 'Well Born.'

Macffarlen (MacFarlane)   From the Lennox district of Scotland; an anglicised form of Mac Pharláin.   The etymology is from the Latin form of Bartholomew one of the Apostles.

Macffay (MacFay) A Redshank surname associated with the Hebridean island of Colonsay. It is an anglicised pet name form of Mac Dhubhidh from the surname Mac Dhuibhshithe which means 'son of the black-haired fairy.'

MacGillione   A difficult anglicised form to decipher, but believed to be from Mac Giolla Eóin a standard Gaelic form of the Scottish Mac Giolla Eáin.

MacGilrouse   Probably another anglicised form of Mac Giolla Rua.

MacGourden (Gordon)   Lowlands; a Mac form of Gordon supposedly from the Cumbric Gour (super) Ddin (fort), but also said to be from old Gaelic Gor (spacious) Dun (fort); a Scottish topographical surname. I could find no sources to support either origin and it may be a habitational name brought to Scotland by the Normans.

MacHutchon (MacCutchen)   Another anglicised form of Mac Úistin; usually from Argyll.

MacIldonagh   An anglicised from Mac Giolla Dhonnchaidh, 'son of the servant of Duncan,' but possibly anglicised from the Gaelic Mac Giolla Domhnaigh, 'son of the servant of the Lord.'

MacIlhome   Anglicised from Mac Giolla Choluim; usually of Argyll origin.

MacIlman   Argyll; from the surname Mac Giolla Mhunna, 'son of the servant of Munn' a saint.

MacIltherne (MacElheron)   An Argyll surname; from the Gaelic Mac Giolla Chiaráin.   In Ulster usually a Clann Dhónaill origin surname.

MacIlwane   Usually an Ayrshire surname; it is an anglicised form of Mac Giolla Bháin.

MacKaine (MacCain, MacKane, MacKean, MacKeen)   From Mac Eáin.   Eáin is a Scottish variation of Eóin which is the Gaelic form of the Latin name Iohannes (John in English).   Several Argyll clans had septs that went by this surname.

MacKaire   In Ulster normally a form of the surname Mac Fhearadhaich, 'son of Fearadach' meaning 'manly.'

MacKan (see MacCan)

MacKeeg   Argyll, Hebrides, and Ulster; from the Gaelic Mac Thaidhg, 'son of the poet.'

MacKeene (see MacKaine)

MacKenily (MacKinley)   This name is probably from Mac Fhionnlaigh, meaning 'son of the fair haired hero.'   It could also be a form of Mac an Leagha, 'son of the physician.'

MacKennye (MacKenny)   Argyll and Lennox; from Mac Cionaodha.   From the given name Cionaodha; a name that dates to ancient times and is believed to be from Cion (respect) and Aodh (fire).

MacKergour   This is probably an anglicised form of Mac Fhearchair meaning 'son of the dear man.'

MacKirdly   Another surname difficult to decipher; possibly from the Gaelic surname Mac Thoirdealbhaigh meaning 'son of Toirdealbhach' or shaped like the Norse god Thor.

MacKyndely (MacKinley; see MacKenily)   This is probably an anglicised form of Mac Fhionnlaigh which picked up the 'd' in the process.

MacLenochan (MacLenachan, MacClenahan)   From Argyll and the western Lowlands;   the Gaelic form is Mac

Leannacháin or 'son of Leannachán' a diminutive of Leannach meaning 'cloaked.'

MacLentock (MacClintock) Argyll and Lennox; from the surname Mac Giolla Fhionntóg or 'son of the servant of the fair hero.' Several Mac Giolla Fhionntóg families settled in Donegal in the 1500s.

MacLynienie A Scottish name associated with Perthshire. It is probably related in etymology to the surname of Mac Giolla Choinnigh, 'son of the servant of Coinneach,' a saint's name; which is also anglicised as MacLinney.

MacMuyre (MacMurry) Found in both the southwest Lowlands, especially in Gallowayshire, and in Argyll and Bute. The Gaelic form is Mac Muireadhaigh from word Muireadhach meaning 'belonging to the sea' that is a mariner.

MacNair Argyll; from the Gaelic Mac an Mhaoir meaning 'son of the steward.'

MacNeron It is difficult to ascertain the Gaelic form of this surname, but it is probably linked to Mac an Airchinn, which is also anglicised MacEnerin, MacNern, and MacNairn. Mac an Airchinn is the shortened form of Mac an Airchinnigh, 'son of the Airchinneach' which was a church official in Gaelic society.

MacNevin alias MacNit (MacNiven) The use of an 'alias' attached to a Gaelic surname was not unusual and often reflected a clan surname. MacNevin was from Argyll and Ayrshire, and is from the Gaelic Mac Naoimhín, 'son of Naoimhín' a diminutive of Naomh, or 'saint.'

MacNichol Argyll and the Hebrides; from the Gaelic surname Mac Niocóil meaning 'son of Nicol' a form of Nicholas.

MacNit (see Naught)

MacPeter A simple Gaelic patronymic, Mac Peadair, 'son of Peter.'

Macquchowne Calhoun with a Mac prefix.

Mactyre (MacIntyre) Argyll; from the Gaelic surname Mac an tSaoir meaning 'son of the carpenter.'

MacWilliam (Williams) From the Gaelic Mac Uilleim, found throughout Scotland.

MacWrick (also MacRirick) Another Gaelic origin surname difficult to decipher; possibly the Gallowayshire name MacCririe, which has several variations. If so the etymology is Norse from Rothrekr meaning 'fame ruler.' This name was adopted by Gaels in both Ireland and Scotland where it is normally seen as Ruairí.

Makee, (MacGee, MacKey) From the Gaelic Mac Aoidh, common surname in Argyll, Islay, and Ulster. The root is Aodh an old Celtic name meaning 'fire.'

Marshell (Marshall) An occupational surname of Norman origin found in Scotland after their settlement there. It is from the old French Mareschal meaning 'one who tended horses.'

Martin Argyll, but also general to Scotland; the Gaelic form is Mac Máirtín.

Michell (Mitchell) From Argyll and the Lowlands; from the Gaelic surname Mac Giolla Mhichil or 'servant of Saint Michael.'

Miller An occupational origin surname from the English miller; a surname often taken by Scots in that profession; in Gaelic Muilleóir.

Moire (Moore) A surname found throughout Scotland and of multiple origins. From the pet name Mór meaning 'big' and from a topographic origin for one who lived near a 'moor' as in a marsh or fen.

Morison (Morrison) Argyll; from the Gaelic Mac Muiris, 'son of Maurice,' a name popularised by the Normans. In the Hebrides the Mac Giolla Mhuire (son of the servant of Mary) families also anglicised their surname as Morrison.

Muntgomery (Montgomery) Scottish of Norman origin; from the French Mont (hill) and Gumaric a Germanic origin name meaning 'man-power.'

Mure (see Moire)

Muthey Lennox and parts of the northern Lowlands; anglicised form of Maitiú (Matthew).

Naught (MacNitt, MacNaught) Argyll; from the surname Mac Neachtain, 'son of Neachtan' or the Pure One. A very old Argyll family linked to Cumbric ancestors.

Niweme I am completely stumped by this odd surname; possibly the English surname Newenham, usually found in Dublin.

Noble Lennox and adjacent areas of the Lowlands; from Norman French via the Latin Nobilis.

Or (Orr) A Scottish surname with two reported origins; from the Gaelic Odhar meaning 'pale' and the Norse Orri meaning 'blackcock.'

Parmenter Lowland; an occupational origin surname from the Norman French Parmentier meaning a maker of trimming and facings.

Patterson A common Scottish surname found in both Argyll and in the Lowlands. The Gaelic form is Mac Páidín, 'son of Padin' a diminutive of Patrick.

Peacock (Pecock) Lowlands; an English surname, but established in Scotland in Medieval times.

Pearce From the Norman French form of Peter; the Gaelic form is Mac Piarais.

Porlerm (Parlan) Lennox; a form of Mac Pharláin.

Porter A Scottish occupational surname for a gatekeeper that is from the French word Portier meaning 'doorman.' General to Scotland including the Highlands.

Pots This is a diminutive of Philpot which is a form of Phillip; Lowland Scottish and numerous in and around Lanarkshire.

Quahone (MacCone) Argyll and general to Scotland; from the Gaelic Mac Eogháin. The letter combination Qua represents a hard C sound in early anglicised forms.

Ralston (Raulston) A Scottish name that originated in Lanarkshire and Renfrewshire. Its origins are from the Norse name Rathulfr (modern form Ralf), from Rath (counsel) and Ulfr (wolf) combined with the Old English Tun meaning 'settlement.'

Ramsey Lowland Scottish; the origin of the surname is disputed, but probably Norse from the 'Hraems Ay' meaning Raven's Island.

Ranckein (Rankin) From the surname Raincín a Gaelic form of Randal. Oral history connects them with Clann Mhic Ghiolla Eáin on Mull.

Reed (Reid) Both Highland and Lowland Scottish origins and from the Lallans word for 'red.' The Gaelic form is Rua.

Reroch A difficult surname to decipher, possibly a spelling of Roach.

Richmoule This rare and unique surname is supposedly an anglicised form of the European forename Ricarda. I cannot say if that is true, but Richmoule, often written Richmul, does appear as a forename in both Colonial America and in the UK.

Richye (Richey) Anglicised form of the Scottish name Mac Risteáird.

Robison (Robinson) From Mac Rob or 'son of Rob' a diminutive of Robert.

Roger (Rodger)   Argyll and the Hebrides; generally an anglicised form of Mac Ruairí a common Gaelic surname throughout the Scottish Gaeltacht. Many with this name are connected to the many Gallóglaigh and Redshanks of Clann Dhónaill.

Rothes A Scottish surname; possibly a habitational surname of Rothes, a glen and village in Aberdeenshire.

Royare (Royer) Scotland; an occupational surname meaning wheelwright from the French Roier.

Scot Generally a Lowland origin surname, but not exclusively, in Gaelic it is Albanach.

Sempell Lowland surname that originated in Renfrewshire. The Probable origin is from a contraction of 'Saint Paul' though some say it originates from the word Simple meaning 'straight forward.'

Smeally The origin of this name is obscure, but probably from the old English words Smael (narrow) and Leah (wood). The name is associated with Lanarkshire.

Smyth (Smith) A common Scottish origin surname. It is the anglicised form of Mac Gabhann meaning the 'son of the smith.'

Snodgarse (Snodgrass)   Originally from Irvine parish in Ayrshire. The name comes from two northern English words Snod meaning 'smooth' and Grass meaning 'grass.'

Speare (Speer) An Ayrshire name; the etymology goes back to the Old French word Espier meaning 'to watch' or 'spy,' i.e. a lookout.

Speney A Scottish name of Norman origin; from the Old French Espinel meaning a copse (small wood) with an etymology going back to the Latin Spina meaning 'thornbush.'

Squire Usually a Lowland surname; it is old French in origin from Escuyer or 'shield bearer.' It became a status surname of one just below the rank of Knight.

Staret (Starret) A toponymic surname taken from the Gaelic Stair Ard which means 'high stepping stones' as in a bridge over a bog, a location in east Ayrshire.

Steavenson (Stevenson) Found throughout Scotland; from the Gaelic surname Mac Steafáin meaning 'son of Stephen.' One Stevenson family was linked to Clann Mhic Ghriogair in the Loch Lomond district and some of the Laggan Redshanks were recruited from that area.

Steward Both Highland and Lowland Scottish; the name is Stiúbhart in Gaelic. The etymology of the name is Old English from Stigeweard, meaning 'hall guardian.' Most Stewards are indigenous to Scotland in origin, but one line at least is from an old Breton family that came with the Normans and settled in Scotland.

Stole An exotic surname that has no known Celtic or Scandinavian origins. There is an English Stole family from Somerset, the etymology of their surname is from the Old English Stan (stony) Wella (spring). But, it is also a Gaelic surname that is recorded on the Isle of Man. The early forms of the Manx Stole family have the Mac prefix which suggest a Gaelic origin, but with an obscure origin and meaning.

Swayne (Swaine) Lowlands and Argyll; the etymology is from the Norse forename Sven which was a term of endearment meaning 'boy.' As a surname it first appears in Lanarkshire.

Symison (Simpson) Lowlands; from 'Simon's son.'

Thomson (Thompson) Lowland and Highlands; a common Scottish surname. The Gaelic forms are Mac Tómais and Mac Thómais.

Thromble (Trumble) A Scottish Lowland name originally from Roxburghshire. It is of Cumbric Celtic origin.

Toes (also Toyes) This is probably the old Yorkshire and Borders surname Toes. Its etymology has two theories, one is it is from the old English word Towe meaning 'tough,' and there is an alternative theory that it comes from the old English Attoe' mean 'ridge dweller.'

Valentyne Scottish surname, usually of Lowland origin; it is written Bhailintín in Gaelic. From the Latin loan word Valens meaning 'strong,' also associated with the saint of the name. It was a medieval forename.

Walker (MacWalker) General to Scotland; it is an occupational name from the old English word Wealcere meaning a cloth worker also called a fuller.

Wan An odd surname held by Black and others to be an anglicised form of Mac Shuibhne. This is probably correct though other Gaelic surnames such as Mac Mhathain could also be phonetically anglicised as 'Wan.'

Watson A common Scottish surname; the Gaelic form is Mac Uait, a pet form of Walter.

White This is an anglicised form of Mac Giolla Bháin meaning 'son of the fair youth.'

Willy (see MacWilliam) A nickname form of Mac Uilleim.

Wilson From the Gaelic Mac Uilliam, common to all of Scotland.

Wood Wood is an anglicised form of several Gaelic surnames that include Coill meaning 'wood,' in the name. It is also a Scottish toponymic for a dweller of a wood from the Latin name de Bosco, meaning 'of the wood.'

Young A numerous surname in Scotland; sometimes a translation of the epithet Óg, meaning 'young.'

Glossary

Breitheamh: The Gaelic word for 'judge;' anglicised as Brehon.

Clann: Gaelic for 'children' or 'offspring;' anglicised as Clan. In Scotland it came to mean a social organization of allied families. The Clann included kinsmen related through both paternal and maternal blood relations. The clann could also include non-blood related families that were allied or long associated with the Clann. Clann structure was found not only in the Scottish Highlands, but also in the Lowlands.

Comharba: The successor of a founder of a church or monastery; anglicised as Co-arb. The comharba was essentially a lay lord within the Church infrastructure in both Ireland and Scotland.

Cruithin: Were tribes of Celts indigenous to eastern Ulster. They were not 'Picts' as they are often described in older texts, but they may have originally been Cumbric speaking and related to Celtic tribes in western Scotland who were called collectively the *Pritani*. Cruthin was the Gaelic term for the Pritani.

Cumbric: The ancient indigenous P-Celtic language of Scotland spoken well into medieval times. It is very was a dialect of Cymraeg (Welsh).

Cymraeg: The Welsh language.

Dál Riada: an early kingdom in northeast Ireland and Argyll.

Diaspora: The dispersion of a people.

Diminutive: This is a pet form of a name with a suffix expressing a smaller form. Example; Seáinín meaning 'little Seán.'

Epithet: a descriptive adjective attached to a name or nickname.

Airchinneach: The hereditary steward of church lands. The position was an ecclesiastical office that functioned as chief officer of the running of church lands. It is often anglicised as Erenagh.

Habitational: A surname derived from the name of a geographic area.

Gaeltacht: The Gaelic speaking areas of Ireland and Scotland.

Gallóglaigh: The elite heavily armoured Gaelic infantry, originally of Scottish origin. The singular form is Gallóglach. Gallóglaigh is anglicised as Galloglass.

Lallans: Originated from northern English dialects and was spoken throughout much of Scottish Lowlands by the 1500s. It has influences from Latin and French due to the Auld Alliance and Dutch and Low German from trade with the Low Countries. It also has many Gaelic loan words. Lallans is often called Ullans in Ulster and the language is still spoken there.

Mac: Gaelic for 'son.'

Mag: A form of Mac often used before a name beginning with a vowel or silent consonant.

Mhic: A form of Mac used in male names to mean descendant of and in a woman's name to show married status.

Nic: The feminine form of Mac.

Ní: The feminine form of Ó.

Ó: Meaning literally 'from,' and in surnames 'the descendants of.' Generally Irish, but some Scots Gaelic families also used Ó forms of their surnames.

Patronymic: A surname deriving from a father or other male ancestor.

Plantation: The confiscation, redistribution, and settlement of lands after the collapse of Gaelic ruled Ulster. It began in 1607 and continued throughout the seventeenth century.

Planter: Common term for an individual that acquired lands during the Ulster Plantation and settlement.

Progenitor: The founder of a family.

Riding Clans: The name given to the reiving families along the Scottish and English Border.

Seneschal: The steward of a medieval lord, the position continued in use into the early modern era in Scotland.

Sept: A group of blood related families living in one area or district.

Taoiseach: the leader or 'chief' of an Irish or Scottish clan.

Toponymic: A surname taken from a geographic place name.

Uí: The genitive form of Ó, found in clan names, such as Clann Uí Dhónaill (clan O'Donnell). It is also used to show unmarried status in a woman's surname that begins with an Ó prefix.

Undertakers: A name given to powerful English and Scottish landowners who undertook the plantation of settlers in Ulster during the Plantation.

Select Bibliography

Calendar of State Papers Relating to Ireland eds Hans Claude Hamilton et al. (24 vols, London, 1860-1911).

Calendar of State Papers Relating to Scotland and Mary, Queen of Scots, 1547-1603 eds J Bain et al. (13 vols, Edinburgh, 1898-1969).

Dawson, Jane E A, *The Politics of Religion In The Age of Mary, Queen Of Scots, The Earl of Argyll and the Struggle for Britain and Ireland*, Cambridge University Press, Cambridge, 2002.

Dawson, Jane E A, *The Campbells are coming! A 16th Century Experience: a Campbell push into the Lennox and Menteith, Drymen* and District Local History Society, 2007.

Heath, Ian, *The Irish Wars 1485-1603*, Osprey Publishing Ltd., London, 1993.

Hill, Michael, *Fire and Sword: Sorley Boy MacDonnell and the Rise of Clan Ian Mor 1538-90*, Oxford University Press, Oxford, 2004.

Hill, Rev. George, *An Historical Account of the MacDonnells of Antrim, Including Notices of other Septs, Irish and Scottish*, Belfast, 1873.

Hill, Rev George, *An Historical Account of the Plantation In Ulster at the Commencement of the Seventeenth Century, 1608-1620.* Scotdisc, electronic copyright 2002.

McLeod, Wilson, *Divided Gaels, Gaelic Cultural Identities in Scotland and Ireland c 1200- c 1650*, Oxford University Press, Oxford, 2004.

Mullin, T.H., *The Ulster Clans*, The University Press, Belfast 1966.

Ó Cleirigh, Lughaidh, *Beatha Aodh Rua O Domhnaill,* Irish Text Society, vol. 42, Educational Company of Ireland. Dublin 1948.

O'Donovan, John ed. *Annala Rioghachta Eireann*, 5 vols, Dublin 1848.

O'Rahilly, Thomas F, *Irish Dialects Past and Present, With Chapters On Scottish and Manx*, Dublin, 1988.

Woulfe, Rev. Patrick, *Sloinnte Gaedheal is Gall*, reprint Kansas City 1992.

Index

Barry R McCain is the administrator of the Ulster Heritage Project. The Project sponsors the Ulster Heritage DNA Project and promotes research into family and general history of the nine counties of Ulster. Mr McCain has a degree in history from Ole Miss. He works as a writer and lives in Oxford, Mississippi.

Ulster Heritage Publishing
PO Box 884
Oxford Mississippi 38655
USA

Made in the USA
Columbia, SC
12 February 2019